Permission to Forget

And Nine Other Root Causes of America's Frustration with Education

Lee Jenkins

ASQ Quality Press
Milwaukee, Wisconsin

American Society for Quality, Quality Press, Milwaukee 53203
© 2005 by ASQ
All rights reserved. Published 2004
Printed in the United States of America

12 11 10 09 08 07 06 05 04   5 4 3 2 1

Library of Congress Cataloging-in-Publication Data

Jenkins, Lee.
  Permission to forget : and nine other root causes of America's
frustration with education / Lee Jenkins.
    p. cm.
  Includes bibliographical references and index.
  ISBN 0-87389-632-7 (soft cover, perfect bound : alk. paper)
  1. Educational evaluation—United States. 2. School management and
organization—United States. 3. Total quality management—United States.
I. Title.

  LB2822.75.J46 2004
  370'.973—dc22   2004014857

ISBN 0-87389-632-7

"From LtoJ" is a trademark of From LtoJ Consulting Group, Inc., and From LtoJ
Software, LLC

Publisher: William A. Tony
Acquisitions Editor: Annemieke Hytinen
Project Editor: Paul O'Mara
Production Administrator: Randall Benson
Special Marketing Representative: David Luth

ASQ Mission: The American Society for Quality advances individual,
organizational, and community excellence worldwide through learning,
quality improvement, and knowledge exchange.

Attention Bookstores, Wholesalers, Schools, and Corporations: ASQ Quality
Press books, videotapes, audiotapes, and software are available at quantity
discounts with bulk purchases for business, educational, or instructional use.
For information, please contact ASQ Quality Press at 800-248-1946, or write to
ASQ Quality Press, P.O. Box 3005, Milwaukee, WI 53201-3005.

To place orders or to request a free copy of the ASQ Quality Press Publications
Catalog, including ASQ membership information, call 800-248-1946. Visit our
Web site at www.asq.org or http://qualitypress.asq.org.

 Printed on acid-free paper

Quality Press
600 N. Plankinton Avenue
Milwaukee, Wisconsin 53203
Call toll free 800-248-1946
Fax 414-272-1734
www.asq.org
http://qualitypress.asq.org
http://standardsgroup.asq.org
E-mail: authors@asq.org

AMERICAN SOCIETY
FOR QUALITY™

With great admiration and love I dedicate this book to Sandy my wife, the mother of our sons Todd and Jim, and the grandmother of Jasmine, Zeke, Samantha, Joshua, Jesse, Jade, and Zeph.

Contents

List of Figures

Preface

If you are looking for a book bashing today's teachers and administrators, this is not the book. *Permission to Forget: And Nine Other Root Causes of America's Frustration with Educaton* outlines problems that were built into American education prior to today's educators graduating from college.

It is well known that society at large creates many problems that children bring to school. For example, as a first-grade teacher prepared to read a farmyard story, she checked with her students to be sure they understood what a "pen" was. One student eagerly raised her hand and explained that a "pen" is where her daddy is. This book does not outline society's ills and how they affect student learning.

Nor does this book attempt to describe the issues that are caused by legislation and can only be corrected by legislation. For example, many students in California have five different school superintendents: one for grades K–8 (or maybe K–6), another one for grades 9–12 (or maybe 7–12), a third one (usually elected) in each county office, a fourth one elected as state superintendent, and a fifth one appointed by the governor (as secretary of education). In addition there are school boards for the first four superintendents. This book does not address the chaos that legislature has the responsibility to fix.

What *Permission to Forget: And Nine Other Root Causes of America's Frustration with Education* does do is describe the deep-seated problems built into America's classrooms that educators can solve. These issues are not on the surface, but are buried in the unconscious operations of daily school life. Lloyd Dobyns and Claire Crawford-Mason wrote, "In order to get quality education, you have to get to the root of the problem. The root of the problem is the poor management system that most schools have in the United States."[1] The management problems described in this book do not distinguish between management of the classroom, management of the school, or management of the school district. Management is management is management regardless of the age of those being managed or the number being managed. Writing about business, Russell Ackoff stated, "Western managers generally believe their poor performance in the global marketplace is due to factors that are out of their control. This belief provides them with a basis for rationalizing their disinclination to make fundamental changes."[2] Writing about educators, Kathleen Kennedy Manzo stated almost the exact same thing. "In too many classrooms . . . achievement levels off, and some students continue to fail. After giving their best, many teachers conclude that other factors are undermining their efforts."[3] Because schools inherit so many problems caused by society and legislatures, employees easily can become disinclined to solving any problems. As this book will outline, however, educators have tremendous power to bring about substantial improvement in schools, in spite of the worst aspects of our society and ineffective legislation.

If you are not an educator, don't be critical—help remove these frustrations from the lives of children and educators. If you are an educator, do not be defensive; you didn't create these problems, but you can remove them from your sphere of influence.

Lee Jenkins
Scottsdale, AZ
lee@fromltoj.com

Introduction

The Juran Institute produced a series of *Quality Minutes* on video in the 1990s.[1] One of them describes a problem with the Jefferson Memorial: the granite was crumbling. What was frustrating to park officials was that none of the other memorials were having this same problem with their granite. So the question was *why?*

Question: *Why* is the granite crumbling on the Jefferson Memorial?

Answer: It is hosed off more than the other memorials.

Question: *Why* is the Jefferson Memorial hosed off more than the other D.C. memorials?

Answer: The Jefferson Memorial has more bird dung.

Question: *Why* does the Jefferson Memorial have more bird dung than the other memorials?

Answer: It has more birds.

Question: *Why* does the Jefferson Memorial have more birds?

Answer: It has more spiders for the birds to eat.

Question: *Why* does the Jefferson Memorial have more spiders than other D.C. memorials?

Answer: It has more flying insects for spiders to eat.

Question: *Why* does the Jefferson Memorial have more flying insects than other D.C. memorials?

Answer: The lights are turned on too soon at the Jefferson Memorial, thus attracting the insects.

Solution: The lights were turned on later and the granite stopped crumbling. By asking *why* enough times, usually at least five, one can find the root causes of problems.

Readers will see that the root causes of today's frustrations with educastion are interrelated and firmly entrenched within America's system of schooling. My book *Improving Student Learning: Applying Deming's Quality Principles in Classrooms* and Quality Press's Continuous Improvement Series were written to solve these root causes.[2] Maybe the books were written in reverse order, but *Permission to Forget: And Nine Other Root Causes of America's Frustration with Education* is published to describe the issues solved by the earlier books.

1

Permission to Forget

Students learn in first grade that they have permission to forget much of what their teachers are teaching. How do they learn this? Six-year-olds learn they have permission to forget through the Friday spelling tests. The process is well-known. New spelling words are assigned on Monday, various learning activities transpire Tuesday through Thursday, cramming takes place on Thursday evening, and a test is given on Friday. Numerous words spelled correctly on Friday are forgotten on Saturday. In fact, one teacher told me she gave the same spelling test two hours later and was shocked to find out how much was already forgotten.

ROOT CAUSE #1
Granting students permission to forget

Any educational institution that encourages cramming is unintentionally giving students permission to forget. Likewise, any initiative that purports to significantly improve education must take cramming out of the equation. This has been accomplished many times by implementing the strategies outlined in *Improving Student Learning: Applying Deming's Quality Principles in Classrooms.*[1] It must be recognized, however, that without my earlier book, many teachers still figured out a classroom system to stop giving permission to forget during the year of their responsibility. So these students

1

waited until summer to forget. This same permission to forget resides in all or nearly all United States schools.

Teachers certainly do not intentionally give this permission. As a former school administrator I've interviewed hundreds of teacher applicants. When asked, "Why do you want to be a teacher?" none ever said, "My professional goal is to help children with their short-term memory." Even though short-term memory is not teachers' aspiration, it becomes the students' cycle—cram, receive a grade, forget, cram, receive a grade, forget.

I don't want to discount the importance of short-term memory. It does come in handy. For example, because of my career of writing and speaking I spend considerable time in hotels. On more than one occasion I have checked in late, gone to my speaking engagement the next day, and returned to the hotel only to have forgotten which room is mine. Invariably, when my short-term memory fails me, there are five people in line to register and I waste time waiting for somebody to inform me of my room number. So short-term memory has a place; it is not, however, the purpose of formal schooling.

EVIDENCE OF PERMISSION TO FORGET ABOUNDS

The evidence that permission to forget is embedded into American education comes from many sources:

• Grade 1–8 math textbooks normally set aside the first one-third of the pages for reteaching of the prior years' content. It is assumed students forget.

• I often ask educators in my seminars what percentage of the school year is spent teaching content students should know prior to entering their course. The answers are typically from 25 percent to 50 percent with some percentages even higher.

• A major school district had a large dispute over when to start the new school year. The educators desired mid-August and the business community advocated the Tuesday after Labor Day. When the educators were asked why starting mid-August was important, they replied that finishing the semester before Christmas was the issue. Then they were asked why finishing the semester before Christmas vacation was important. Educators replied that if finals are given before vacation, students perform much better than if finals are given after vacation. It seems that educators don't blush when confronted with the fact that students don't even remember for two weeks what they are taught. As I said in the preface, this book is not about bashing educators. Permission to forget is so ingrained in the thinking of educators it is not given a second thought.

• A sixth-grade student, his father, and his teacher are having a conference. Teacher says, "Dad, your son needs to learn his times tables." Dad, looking over at son, says, "I thought we did this last year." Son replies, "I didn't know you meant learn them like *that*."

• A second-grader brings home his spelling words with a couple of misspelled words. Mom states, "I see you did pretty well, but you missed two words. Let's work on the words you missed." Son replies, "No, Mom, I don't want to." "Why not?" Mom asks. "These are important words that you misspelled." "Well, Mom," says son, "these words are never coming up again. I don't need to know how to spell them."

• California curriculum leaders had a great concept for organizing U.S. history content. It doesn't work, but the concept is exemplary. Curriculum designers were attempting to overcome the problem of fifth-, eighth-, and eleventh-grade U.S. history classes all starting with European exploration and ending about the time of the Civil War. The same content is taught three times. The proposed solution was to teach fifth grade up to the American Revolution, teach history from the U.S. Constitution to 1900 in the eighth grade, and continue up to the current time in the eleventh grade. Why doesn't the concept work? Students forget the prior taught history so eighth and eleventh grade teachers have little residue of knowledge from which to build.

In a 1998 *Kappan* article, "Seventeen Reasons Why Football Is Better than High School," Herb Childress wrote, "Students picked up enough information to pass the test, did their work well enough to get the grade, and then totally forgot whatever it can be said they had learned."[2]

Ronald A. Wolk wrote, "I took two years of high school algebra, geometry, and trigonometry, and forgot most of it before the ink on my diploma was dry."[3]

Edward Deci has researched this subject. He reported, "People employing tests to motivate learning are unwittingly defeating the desire to learn in those people they are attempting to help . . . It seems that when people learn with the expectation of being evaluated, they focus on memorizing facts, but they don't process the information as fully, so they don't grasp the concepts as well . . . those who had learned expecting to be tested had forgotten much more . . . Evidently, they memorized the material for the test, and when the test was over, they pulled the plug and let it drain out."[4] Students know their algebra II teacher will not demand they remember the content they were taught last year in geometry.

FINANCIAL AND INSTRUCTIONAL IMPLICATIONS OF PERMISSION TO FORGET

The instructional implications of no longer giving students permission to forget are obvious. The financial impact is huge. The cost to operate America's public schools is over $2 billion per day. Many propose adding 30 or more days per year of schooling. The cost for these 30 days is $60 billion per year. It is safe to assume that at least 30 days a year are currently devoted to rework because students have permission to forget. Eliminating permission to forget will come at a cost because staff development is not free. Staff development investments are slim, however, compared to adding days of instruction.

In this volume I am not rewriting the details of *Improving Student Learning: Applying Deming's Quality Principles in Classrooms,* but will state a few of the basics. When permission to forget is denied, students are always assessed on long-term memory, never short-term memory. For example, students in eighth-grade physical science are responsible for the information and performance content of seventh-grade life science and sixth-grade earth science. Every nongraded feedback and every graded evaluation draw from the entire previous year's content plus the current year's content. Students are informed in every grade that the expectations for their current grade are not going away. They need to file the knowledge away in their long-term memory because the content will come up over and over and over. Weekly assessments in eighth-grade science, for example, might be 10 questions from eighth grade plus four questions from seventh grade and four questions from sixth grade.

EDUCATION AND BUSINESS SHARE THE SAME PROBLEM

Probably the statement that most irritates me in regard to education is that "education needs to be run more like a business." The inference is that business does everything right and education does it all wrong, when, in fact, there are numerous examples of poor business practices. One example where I would have loved to have been more businesslike, was to be legally able to select the building contractors in town known to have a great reputation. However, state law forced me to accept low bid for construction projects. In one such example of a low bid, the heating/air conditioning contractor did not wrap the elbows of the pipes, only the straight portion of the pipes. When confronted by the inspector, he replied, "It didn't say wrap the elbows, only the pipes." Over and over the low-bid process rips off school systems. So, certainly freedom to select honest, quality contractors is one of the ways education could be more businesslike. Nevertheless, the blanket statement that children can be treated the way a car going down the assembly line can be treated is false and overly simplistic. So I was listening acutely when W. Edwards Deming addressed this topic.

Deming stated that the solution for education is *not* to be more businesslike because the root causes of problems in government, business, and education are all the same. In his seminars he often criticized business for making short-term decisions, such as decisions that are good for the quarterly report but bad for the business overall. For example, he described a manufacturing company that was near the end of the quarter and was about to show a loss. Pressure was on to ship orders before the end of the quarter to show a profit. One piece was missing from a supplier, but it was decided to ship anyway. This way the shipped products could be counted as accounts receivable and thus a profit could be reported for the quarter. Three weeks into the next quarter the manufacturer flew representatives to the various locales that had purchased the product to install the missing piece. This was done, of course, at great cost to the company's long-term financial health.

Suggestions for business to stop their short-term thinking are abundant. For example, Myron Tribus writes, "One of the most important changes that could be made, without cost and at once, would be to make the retirement benefits of executives depend on the earnings of the company after retirement."[5] Tribus is attacking the issue of business executive "cramming" to get the stock price up prior to their final "exam," which for them is their retirement package.

So, taking to heart Deming's position that the root causes of educational problems are the same as the root causes of business problems, I began to search for short-term thinking in education. What about education is the same? It didn't take long to realize that education's prime example of short-term thinking is cramming. It is endemic.

Deming wrote, "No number of short-term successes in short-term problems will ensure long-term success." The sentence for education is, "No number of successes on chapter tests will ensure success on high-stakes, standardized exams."

When teachers first start the process of assessing students only on long-term memory, some parents have a concern. The issue is that their son or daughter is not answering 100 percent of the questions as formerly done with short-term chapter quizzes. When educators explain that they are overcoming the cramming/forget cycle, however, parents are understanding and supportive. They know from their own educational experience the futility of cramming.

HIGH STANDARDS *AND* HIGH SUCCESS RATES

My seminars begin with a comparison of a central business issue with education's number one issue. The business issue is the requirement to have higher quality and lower cost at the same time. Beginning with Deming's teaching in Japan in 1950, the world of business has slowly come to believe this is possible. Education's requirement, because of No Child Left Behind legislation, is to have both higher standards and higher success rates at the same time. Just as business assumed that higher quality meant higher costs, education assumed that higher standards meant lower success rates. Well Deming proved through Japanese competition that higher quality and lower costs were possible and education is embarking on the same journey.

Congress has mandated that education is to accomplish in 14 years what business is still attempting to accomplish after 50 years. Business is improving, but has not arrived yet. For example, *Business Week* reports, "For new cars, U.S. automakers have narrowed the quality gap with foreign brands, but they're still not in the top tier." It then reports defects per 100 vehicles with Toyota, BMW, and Honda above average and General Motors, Ford, and DaimlerChrysler below average. GM, Ford, and Chrysler's 2003 quality is exactly where Toyota, BMW, and Honda were in 2002.[6] This superior quality is occurring at the same time that Toyota and Honda are manufacturing their cars in three hours less time than General Motors, four hours less than Ford and six hours less than DaimlerChrysler.[7] For U.S. business leaders to convince legislators that they they have the answer to education's woes is inaccurate at best and possibly dishonest. Business leaders have not solved their short-term thinking problems and are not assisting education with its short-term cramming issues.

PLEASE BLAME PERMISSION TO FORGET FOR POOR RESULTS

It won't be long after readers have completed this chapter that they will pick up yet another article such as *USA Today's* headline story on Friday, May 10, 2002, "Kids Get 'Abysmal' Grade in History." The article goes on to explain that 57 percent of seniors could not perform at even the basic level, 32 percent performed at the basic level, 10 percent at grade-level work, and one percent were advanced or superior.[8] It is my hope that when the next article is printed, readers will not think poorly of the history (or whatever other subject is named) teachers but remember that everyone (students and teachers) are performing exactly as the system dictates.

Teachers have taught the history that is tested on the national exams. Students have answered similar questions for their grades. The system has not required that students remember the course content beyond the end of the course, and guess what? They don't! Permission to forget is the norm.

CONCLUSION

Educators are held accountable for students' long-term memory as measured by standardized exams and performance in the university, the military, or in other occupations. Students, however, are held accountable for their short-term memory as measured by chapter tests, and Friday quizzes on the current week's curriculum. The education system has a major disconnect.

Key Recommendation

Seventy percent of every nongraded weekly quiz and 70 percent of every graded exam should include questions from the current course and 30 percent of every nongraded weekly quiz and every graded exam should be from the content of prior courses. For example, an algebra II quiz or exam should be 70 percent algebra II and 30 percent algebra I and geometry. In schools with an interdisciplinary curriculum in which all strands of math are taught each year, 70 percent of junior level exams should be from the junior level course and 30 percent from the prior two years' content.

This recommendation is true for all subjects. For example:

- Eighth-grade history exams should be composed of 70 percent eighth-grade U.S. history and 30 percent fifth-grade U.S. history.

- Eighth-grade physical science exams should be composed of 70 percent eighth-grade science plus 30 percent sixth-grade earth science and seventh-grade life science. (The exact sequence of science courses changes from state to state, but the concept is the same.)

- Ninth-grade English exams should be 70 percent ninth-grade content and 30 percent middle school content.

- Third-grade spelling tests should be 70 percent third-grade words and 30 percent first- and second-grade words.

> J. M. Juran states "In the U.S.A. about a third of what we do consists of redoing work previously 'done.' "[9]

NO

Cramming

Short-term memory

YES

Learning

Long-term memory

2

The Wrong Statistics

ost of the educational attention six-year-olds receive for their
accomplishments revolves around their newfound ability to read
print. In general, children enter first grade reading their name, the
names of family members and a few friends, some popular commercial
signs, and a few other basic words. They leave first grade being able to read
simple books.

Not as noticed is the growth of six-year-olds in mathematics. At the
beginning of first grade children have little knowledge of place value.
The task, "Place these numbers (103, 30, 16, 61, 98, and 3) in order from
smallest to largest" is quite difficult. To a six-year-old, 16 and 61 seem
the same and 98 should be larger than 103. After all, 98 has big numbers
and 103 has only small numbers.

Nevertheless, with proper instruction and appropriate, made-to-scale
materials, first-graders do learn how to place numbers in order from smallest
to largest. Sadly, most of education's published statistics are based on knowledge of first-grade mathematics: place these school results in order from
highest to lowest.

Classroom, school, school district, state department of education, federal, and international statistics are usually based on ranking. Learning how
to rank is significant in a child's mathematical growth and is the foundation
for athletic statistics. We really do care who is in first place in athletics.
Athletics is fun; it's a game.

ROOT CAUSE #2
Education adopted the wrong statistics

Education is not a game and the statistics appropriate and desirable for games are inappropriate and undesirable for nonathletic events. The responsibility of educators is to maximize winners and minimize losers. This is exactly the opposite of the aim in athletics: maximize losers and create one winner. I hope readers of this book do not take this text as a criticism of athletics, but understand it as a compliment. Athletics got it right (except for collegiate football); early on, organizers chose the appropriate statistics for its purpose. Education got it wrong. For example, the headline for a *Sacramento Bee* article on February 21, 2003, was "State Releases New Rankings for Schools." Governor Gray Davis is quoted in the article as saying, "It (the ranking) reflects our belief that all students in all schools deserve challenging academic content that will prepare them for success in school and beyond."[1] I believe that former Governor Davis does want what he stated, but his ranking of schools has predetermined that most of California's students must attend loser schools. Only a few can attain the highest-ranking. What Governor Davis and others need is the understanding written by Douglas Reeves. "Either we evaluate students compared to a clear standard or we compare them to each other; there is no third alternative."[2] When clear standards are present, ranking is no longer necessary.

Ranking will produce a bell-shaped curve in most instances. The bell-shaped curve works for athletics; major league baseball teams can be ranked by games won and then graphed. Figure 2.1 is a bell-shaped graph of the 2003 Major League Baseball results. This makes sense because the number of games is limited, and when one team wins, another loses. The success of one student, however, does not subtract from the success of another student—unless educators force a bell-shaped curve upon their students.

For illustration purposes, visualize 100 students who are in eighth-grade math and are graded on the curve. Let's assume that 70 students receive As, Bs, and Cs and are assigned to algebra in ninth grade. These 70 students are graded on the curve (ranked) and 40 move on to geometry in tenth grade. In geometry, the 40 are again ranked and 16 move on to algebra II. When the ranking occurs again there are between four and eight in calculus. Readers should calculate the math dropout rate for their school system. How many first-graders are there and how many calculus students? Few places have

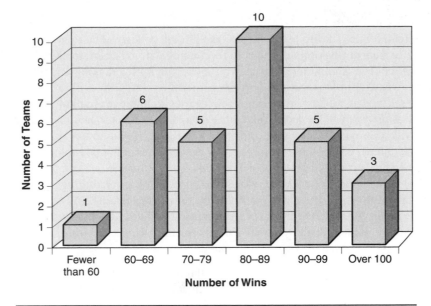

Figure 2.1   Major league baseball results in 2003.

over 10 percent of their students in calculus. I estimate the U.S. math dropout rate at 90 percent. This phenomena does not occur because math teachers are consciously discouraging students. The bell curve is below the surface and unchallenged, just like the Jefferson Memorial lights described in the introduction. One significant by-product of the bell-curve mentality is a shortage of mathematicians in the United States. One can visit almost any high-tech corporation and find that the United States has imported many of the employees in the positions requiring in-depth knowledge of mathematics.

The bell curve is not faring much better in business. "In companies across the country, from General Electric to Hewlett-Packard, such grading systems—in which all employees are ranked against one another and grades are distributed along some sort of bell curve—are creating a firestorm of controversy. In the past 15 months, employees have filed class-action suits against Microsoft and Conoco as well as Ford, claiming that the companies discriminate in assigning grades."[3]

I recognize that schools are under pressure to rank high school students. A high school student in Glendale, Arizona is pressuring her school district, for example, to change the ranking rules. "She believes the class rank is a key factor in college admission."[4] The aim of schools—create as many winners as possible—is in direct conflict with the policies of some "elite" universities. What should schools do? I suggest that school staffs make it clear that their primary aim is to create as many winners as possible. However, in a desire to hurt no students in the college admission process, give students the option to sign up for ranking. "If you desire to be ranked, for college admission purposes, you must sign up for ranking and attend the ranking rules meeting. The rules for calibrating GPA will be clearly explained as well as the penalties for cheating to improve a ranking. If you sign up, you will be ranked with other so inclined students and this ranking will be provided to assist with college admission. If you do not sign up to be ranked, you will not be ranked. We will do everything possible to help create as many winners as possible, ranked or not ranked."

The silliest of rankings is the annual *U.S. News* ranking of colleges and universities. The ranking is based on several factors, the SAT scores of incoming freshmen being the biggest factor.[5] I will not attempt to restate the superb research done by James Fallows for the *Atlantic Monthly,* but will provide a few quotes:

> "Penn's improvement (in ranking) through the 1980's was due largely to its shrewd recruitment and marketing efforts.

> "It (Penn) also made unusually effective use of the most controversial tactic in today's elite-college admissions business: the 'early decision' program.

> "From a college's point of view, the most important fact about early decision is that it provides a way to improve a college's selectivity and yield simultaneously, and therefore to move the school up on the national-ranking charts.

> "The admissions office can affect this (ranking) directly, by giving SAT scores extra weight in its decisions—and surprising new evidence suggests that many offices are doing so."

If *U.S. News* has it correct and our universities should be ranked on the basis of freshman SAT scores, then we should rank K–12 schools on kindergarten readiness scores and businesses on the salary of newly hired employees. Imagine this: University presidents, all of whom have completed a PhD dissertation requiring extensive knowledge of statistics, have achieved the highest status in their profession and are now victim to *U.S. News's* use of first-grade mathematics. Even worse, the ranking is dependent largely on input, not output. At least the automotive ranking was based on output, not the quality of the purchased steel (input).

The public can always depend on annual articles on the ranking of states based on SAT and ACT scores. In a state where few high school seniors take the SAT test and many take the ACT, one can expect the annual "woe is us" article when the ACT scores are published and the "trumped the national average" article when the SAT scores are released.[6] And then there's the simple sentence included at the end of one article, "SAT scores remained generally flat and Georgia ranks 50th in the nation."[7]

Newspapers should publish a scatter diagram with the two scoring variables of SAT results and percentage of students taking the exam. For Oklahoma to state it "trumped the national average" with eight percent of its graduating seniors taking the SAT and for Georgia to be blasted by its press when 68 percent of the students took the exam is misleading and causes poor legislative decisions. Georgia is clustered with a dozen other states with 55 percent to 75 percent of its recent high school graduates taking the SAT. Figure 2.2 is a scatter diagram of the 2003 SAT math results. If newspapers would publish both trend data, showing the past 20 years for their state, and also publish the scatter diagram showing all states, the public could be spared from incomplete, misleading articles. Ideally, newspapers would publish the ACT and SAT articles on the same day avoiding the teeter-totter pair of reports.

The scatter diagram allows the reader to compare two variables. For SAT purposes, variable one is the SAT score shown in Figure 2.2 as the *y* axis. Variable two, on the *x* axis, displays the number of students taking the exam. Fifty dots, one for each state, are on the scatter diagram. In the upper left corner of the graph are clustered the states with high scores, but low participation rates. At the far right are the states with the opposite

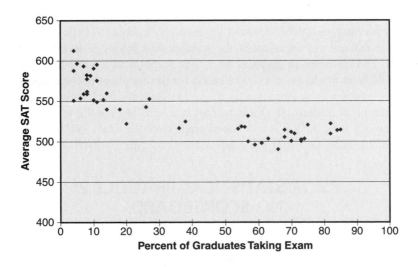

Figure 2.2   A scatter diagram of 2003 math SAT results.

data: lower scores but much higher participation. Readers can see for themselves the almost perfect correlation between percent of graduates taking the exam and the average SAT score for the state. They can also see that none of the 50 states have either high participation/high scores or low participation/low scores.

I had always assumed that "mirror" was a reasonable synonym for statistics until I heard Deming. He stated that one selects the type of statistics necessary for the purpose at hand. So, since the purpose of education is to create as many winners as possible, schools need different statistics. The National Research Council report, without mentioning statistics, clearly states the aim. "When success is defined in terms of competitive status with others, only a few students can be successful. However, when individual growth is the criterion for success, then all students can experience success regardless of their comparative status."[8] Using different words, Douglas Reeves states, "Ultimately the leader does not need to know who beat whom, but only the percentage of students who meet or exceed standards."[9] In order to achieve the aim of success for all, different statistics are imperative.

POOR STATISTICAL PRACTICE 1: NOT ASPIRING TO A J CURVE

It is often easier for people to know what is wrong than to discern the new concept. Such is the case with the bell curve. Many times I've read and heard comments similar to what I've just written about the evils of the bell curve without any mention of the concept and language to replace the bell. The replacement graph is the J. The graph at the end of any course should be in the shape of a J. The bell is for the middle of the year because some students learn more rapidly than other students, but by year's end all or almost all students should have met standards leaving the graph in the shape of a J. Figure 2.3 is a J-shaped graph from the totals for five periods of middle school math. It was made at the end of the 2003–04 school year.

POOR STATISTICAL PRACTICE 2: NO SCOREBOARD

In the article entitled, "Seventeen Reasons Why Football Is Better Than High School," reason 4 is, "In football, a player can let the team down." The bell curve is poor statistical practice 1; the lack of a scoreboard is poor statistical practice 2. The teacher has only a series of numbers that provide

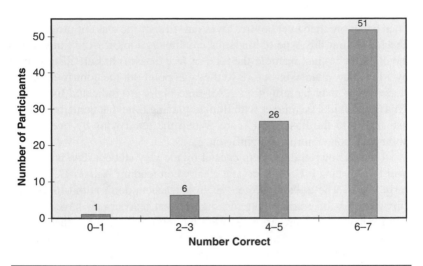

Figure 2.3   Five periods of middle school math with an end-of-year J curve.

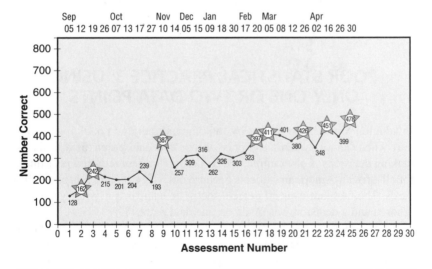

Figure 2.4   Five periods of middle school math with the class run chart displaying total correct for all students together.

little insight into either the teacher or the students and whether or not learning is improving. The class run chart, Figure 2.4, on the other hand, provides evidence to students regarding their contribution to the team. Students can say, "The class total went up five higher than ever before, and

I had one more than ever before. I was one-fifth of the class improvement." Teachers using this type of statistics continually look for the times when the class (or in this example the total of five classes) has an all-time best by a few more than ever before so they can point out the contribution of a student who may be struggling. (All-time highs are indicated by a star.) This is not unlike the player with limited playing time that contributes only two points to the basketball score. When the team wins by one or two points, the contribution is significant.

I have known the problem caused by the way student data is kept for over thirty years. It became crystal clear when reading *Wad-Ja-Get?* in the early 1970s. The authors wrote, "Even if teachers don't admit to using a curve, studies of grading patterns suggest that teachers do have them in mind. They usually are not supported by any rationale other than whim. One major argument against this practice is that the aim of education is to establish reasonable objectives that are within the grasp of most students. So, hopefully, every student will do well, and there will be no need to give a prescribed percentage of low grades."[10] I'm convinced that the eloquence of this book is what caused me to fully appreciate in 1992 Deming's suggestion, described in *Improving Student Learning*, that provided an alternative to the bell curve.

POOR STATISTICAL PRACTICE 3: USING ONLY ONE OR TWO DATA POINTS

In addition to the harm caused by ranking and the grade book, people are hurt when school systems use only one or two data points as a basis for making decisions. For example, a Texas school system required peer tutors for all African-American students because only 48.4 percent met state standards. The fact that over 50 percent met state standards in prior years was ignored and a decision was made on one data point.[11]

It is very common for educators and journalists to make errors based on two data points—last year and this year. Figures 2.5 to 2.8 show four figures that are test results from four hypothetical schools for the years 1 to 5. In all four schools, 52 percent of students met state standards in Year 4 and 49 percent met standards in Year 5. With only the data available to journalists for Year 4 and Year 5, the stories in four communities would be almost identical. When trends are studied over time, however, there are four completely different stories. The time for educators to approach journalists regarding the reporting of trends is when the results are positive. If educators only ask for the trend data to be published when their scores go down, their advice is suspect. It looks as if they are attempting to sugarcoat a bad

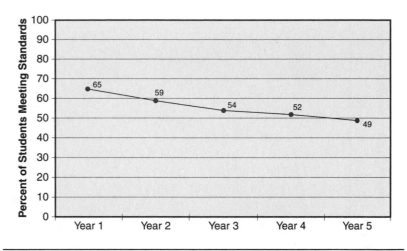

Figure 2.5   Test results from the first hypothetical school.

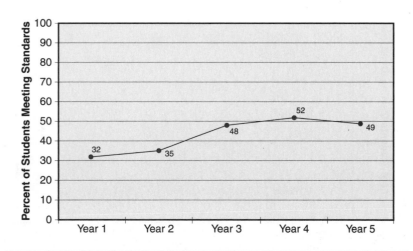

Figure 2.6   Test results from the second hypothetical school.

year. When educators request that trend data be published, however, even though it takes away some of the two-year glory, then journalists will be more likely to publish trends.

Even when educators come to understand the power of studying patterns and trends, state boards of education change the tests. If people making the decisions regarding which tests to purchase believe the local district employees are lazy, then it makes perfectly good sense to change the tests as

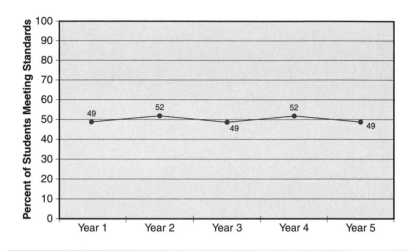

Figure 2.7   Test results from the third hypothetical school.

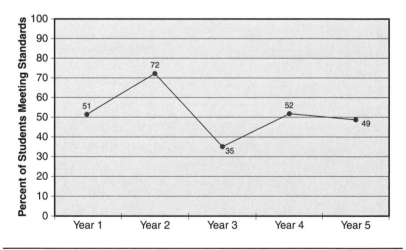

Figure 2.8   Test results from the fourth hypothetical school.

often as possible because any test results can be ranked. If, however, one believes the people are diligently performing their duties, then patterns and trends matter. Changing tests, based on low bid, is a significant problem for the field of education. As one educator reported to the *Indystar,* "Previously we could track our progress from year to year. Now we're back to a new baseline year." The journalists wrote a whole article stating that comparisons could not be made because the tests changed, then went on to compare the

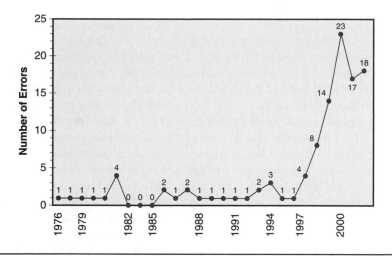

Figure 2.9   This chart shows the number of human errors by the testing industry found in standardized tests.
Source: National Board for Educational Testing and Public Policy.

2002 results to the 2003 results. At the end of the article they inserted a quote showing that the comparisons were not valid and then concluded with another invalid comparison.[12] (I am not inferring that Indiana changed exams based on low bid; their change was a significant alignment of assessment with standards. I am also aware, however, of test changes made in many states that did not bring the assessments any closer to state standards. The five-year contract with one test publisher expired, so bids were received and another off-the-shelf test was purchased.)

What does the public deserve? It deserves data over time such as that provided by the National Board for Educational Testing and Public Policy. Its graph, Figure 2.9, shows the number of reported errors on standardized tests for over 25 years. Now readers can draw their own conclusions from the patterns and not be subjected to articles with only one or two data points.[13]

POOR STATISTICAL PRACTICE 4: THE DATA ARE TOO LATE

Former New York City Mayor Rudy Giuliani wrote, "The main frustration with the state of policing was that each set of statistics was already obsolete by the time it was available. Examining the numbers annually or even quarterly wasn't accomplishing anything in real time. By the time a pattern of crime was noticed, it would have changed."[14]

This paragraph can be rewritten for education almost word for word. "The main frustration with the state of education was that each set of statistics was already obsolete by the time it was available. Examining the numbers annually or even quarterly wasn't accomplishing anything in real time. By the time a pattern of failure was noticed, the student body changed."

In the early part of this century, educators are investing millions to provide data. One of the saddest expenses is quarterly data. Traditionally, education only had annual data, so it seems like quarterly data would be a great improvement. Wrong. Data, if teachers are to use it, are needed weekly or biweekly. Once in a while, data on topics like reading fluency can be obtained monthly and be of value, but this is an exception. The time allocation is 12 to 15 minutes per week per subject or period. With this structure, data can actually be timely. Teachers and students can make many midcourse adjustments to impact learning. Sometimes these adjustments include reteaching particular content or allocating less time to some topics because of quick learning on the part of students. Repeatedly, I hear from educators who have implemented weekly review/preview of end-of-the-year standards that they are able to place learning expectations in students' long-term memory and save six to eight weeks of instructional time during the academic year. Again, the details are provided in *Improving Student Learning: Applying Deming's Quality Principles in Classrooms.*

POOR STATISTICAL PRACTICE 5: THE DATA ARE FOR REACTION AND NOT FOR PREVENTION

Giuliani also writes, "First crime statistics were collected and analyzed every single day, to recognize patterns and potential trouble before it spread."[15] Whenever it is announced that I'll be conducting a seminar in a particular city, teachers see that the topic will include a great deal of data. They have a very hard time, prior to the seminar, believing that two days spent with data could really be of help. Two days on methods of teaching they understand, but data seem like a waste of time.

Why would they think this? It is because every other data experience they have had contains two major problems. The first is that it is usually old data from students they are no longer teaching and the second is that tables of numbers are not graphed in a manner allowing them to glean insights.

When teachers come to understand the power of the histogram showing the class moving from an L to a J, plus other equally powerful graphs, they see, maybe for the first time, that data are used to prevent learning problems. See Figure 2.10 for a beginning of the year L and an end of the

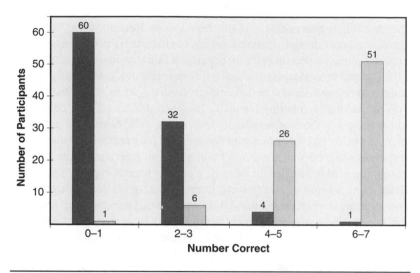

Figure 2.10 Middle grade mathematics with an L in the beginning of the year and a J at the end of the year.

year J. Students in these middle school classrooms were assessed each week on seven randomly selected, end-of-the-year standards.

POOR STATISTICAL PRACTICE 6: NUMERICAL GOALS WITH ARBITRARY NUMBERS

One of the saddest conversations I've ever had in education was with a lamenting principal. Her school test scores improved by over five percent the second year of a particular exam. The next year there was another five percent improvement. On the fourth year they improved another three percent above the previous year. This should have been cause for great joy. It was not. Why?

The governor had set the arbitrary goal of five percent improvement each and every year. If he had read Guiliani's book, he might have seen the folly in this decision. The data are used to "compare the current year's total with the prior year's and show percentage change."[16]

Elsewhere in his book, Guiliani recounts how the chancellor of New York City Schools promised a five percent to 10 percent increase in reading scores. "Well, scores did improve—by 3.6 percent. The press remembered the five to 10 percent promise. The press reported it under the headline

'Student Math Scores' Gain Is the Smallest in Recent Years.' What was actually a boost in reading scores, which could have helped the morale of a broken system, ended up deflated because it failed to meet expectations."[17]

The real numerical goal is to score better than last year. Small gains are improvement and should be celebrated. Guiliani wrote, "No matter what you're tracking, comparing results to previous indicators, then demanding improvement is the best way to achieve anything."[18] Some will argue that there is a crisis and we cannot wait for small incremental improvements. My response is that over 30 years ago I was sitting in meetings where administrators required us teachers to write five percent annual improvement goals. If the mere writing of five percent improvement goals had brought about five percent improvement, this book would not be necessary. American schools would be over 400 percent better than they were 30 years ago! (It is not 150 percent better, because the improvement is compounded.)

The setting of arbitrary goals is guaranteed to discourage many people because it takes away the joy of actual improvement and accomplishes nothing. Deming wrote, "A numerical goal accomplished nothing. Only the method is important, not the goal. Work on a method for improvement of a process. By what method?"[19] I fully recognize that No Child Left Behind (NCLB) legislation has mandated arbitrary numbers. As stated in the preface, this book is not about the problems caused by legislation. Nevertheless, school administrators do have the responsibility to display and celebrate improvement, even if the amount of improvement does not equal NCLB's arbitrary goals.

POOR STATISTICAL PRACTICE 7: THE REPORT CARD

A cultural conflict is ahead with No Child Left Behind. But first, following are the improvement steps taking place in the United States because of NCLB and the focus on standards.

Schools are establishing the essential information and performance standards necessary for each grade and subject. The standards are being set very precisely. Prior to standards and NCLB this was unnecessary. The responsibility of the teacher was to teach the content of the textbook, give exams, and place the results on a bell-shaped curve having the appropriate number of As, Bs, Cs, Ds, and Fs.

Schools are coordinating the standards between grade levels. Knowing nouns and verbs, for example, is a standard at only one grade level. Schools are determining the appropriate grade level and then holding students responsible for remembering prior grade standards as they progress toward graduation. Schools are accepting their new accountability for students to meet these standards. There are certainly struggles, but progress is being made.

The conflict involves statistics. Under the pre-NCLB paradigm, teachers were directed to compare students against students. Now they are being asked to compare students against standards. The essential question from parents to teachers will not be, "How is my child doing compared to other students?" but "How is my child doing compared to standards?" Parents will desire to know how their children are performing compared to other children, but this knowledge will become secondary to comparison against standards.

Traditional report cards communicate clearly that many will be left behind. A standards-based report card communicates that learning is a journey. The aim is not to rank the students, but to have no child left behind because all met grade-level standards.

POOR STATISTICAL PRACTICE 8: AWARDS USED TO RANK AND LEAVE MOST BEHIND

It may not seem like an award assembly has anything to do with statistics, however, educators do use some form of tabulation or numbers to determine which students receive the rewards and which are ignored. A great deal of time is used to make these decisions, which communicate to most children that they don't quite have what it takes to be successful. I could never describe the problem as well as Edward H. Johnson, a Georgia-based business consultant and former president of Atlanta Deming Study Group, did regarding his experience as a social science fair judge. His letter to Laura Bush is shown in the sidebar on page 24.

As Edward Deci says, "With a competition, the second-place person—who may have missed only by a hair—is a loser."[20]

NCLB stands for No Child Left Behind. The letters more accurately should be MCLB—Most Children Left Behind. America has a long ways to go to achieve even HCLB—Half of the Children Left Behind. Readers of this statement who teach second grade will have a difficult time believing what I write for they know full well that almost all of their students are succeeding. To understand this statement one must look at the system after 13 years—one or two students, from the starting kindergarten class of 23, are left behind each year.

May 27, 2003
First Lady Laura Bush
The White House
1600 Pennsylvania Avenue NW
Washington, DC 20500

Dear Mrs. Bush:

Some years ago I once accepted an invitation to be a judge in a local middle school's Social Science Fair Contest. Wanting to know what I had gotten myself into, I made it a point to review the 30 or so student entries on display well before the judging got underway. To my surprise, I found each entry's content noteworthy in spite of a few grease spots here and there. Each entry stood as "a class act," I said to a teacher nearby. Pleased, the teacher repeated my comment to other teachers.

Soon after the judging got underway, an odd uneasiness formed in my gut. For some reason not yet in my conscious, I was fretting having to contribute to judging one entry "First Place Winner," one "Second Place Winner," and one "Third Place Winner."

A day after the contest, the odd uneasiness in the gut gave way to this nagging question: What wisdom was there in deliberately making losers of so many children?

Sometimes we are fortunate to encounter opportunities that allow us to examine our values and the things we do and hold dear. In the face of such opportunities we will either defend our values or, with eyes wide open and ears clicked on, attempt to learn and develop and change for the better.

That day, the Social Science Fair Contest opened my eyes and forced my ears on so that I might experience learning competition among youngsters in a new, revealing way. I suspect it was the unmistakable expressions of dejection on the faces of the contest losers that made me see and hear differently. Even the second- and third-place winners strained to put on a happy face, which showed me they too saw themselves as losers. Moreover, I plainly saw that the first place winner had attained recognition at the expense of all the other contestants, a God-awful lesson for a child to learn about learning and, perhaps more importantly, how to esteem others.

Overall, I saw the event as that of adults inculcating within children the adults' win–lose values based seemingly on the belief system that even in school, as in life elsewhere, there must be winners and losers, that a few children deserve to win and most children deserve to lose.

Left wondering how many potential social scientists I had helped derail that day, I reluctantly took responsibility for my part in the competition then asked my inner being for forgiveness. In the end, that day was a day of personal transformation. Consequently, I vowed to advocate against and never again be a party to events that aim to turn kids into losers through arbitrary and capricious non-sports competition.

Case in point: a recent year's celebration of Dr. Martin Luther King, Jr.'s birthday and legacy featured middle schoolers in a "Martin Luther King, Jr. Essay Writing Contest." Where is the wisdom in turning the many children into essay writing losers in the name of Dr. King? I suggest there is none. When did Dr. King ever stand to make anybody a loser? I suggest he never did. An Essay Writing Collaboration in which every student would aim to contribute to every other student's success and joy in writing would have been a far more fitting celebration of Dr. King's birth and legacy.

Legislators, boards of education, and top school administrators must come to examine their contributions to the nearly imperceptible yet continual demoralization of K–12 school students by way of learning competition. A very real unintended consequence is the near complete destruction of children's intrinsic motivation for learning in school. To protect themselves, if only in their own eyes, many kids will drop out of school rather than submit to loser status . . .

Clearly, today's world demands as many winners as possible, not as many losers as possible. By managing them as athletic-style competitions with attendant rankings and such, our K–12 educational systems cannot possibly help produce the many winners the world needs.

Edward H. Johnson

Source: Personal correspondence from Edward H. Johnson. Used with permission.

POOR STATISTICAL PRACTICE 9: MAKING EVERYTHING A CONTEST

Music is another academic discipline ripe for discussion. As a school superintendent I know it was always reported to the school board when one of our music groups placed first in the regional or state festivals. We never reported to the school board when we lost. The school board approved the field trip and nothing was reported back except maybe a quick e-mail that the students returned safely. I've asked music instructors how students feel when losing at a music festival. The reaction is known to all. I've also asked if there is a way to know if all of this year's choirs are performing at a higher level than the collective choirs from prior years and was told yes. Let's think this through. What is the aim of music festivals? What is the purpose of bringing together musicians from various schools? Is it to discourage or uplift?

POOR STATISTICAL PRACTICE 10: USE OF AVERAGE

An improvement brought about by the NCLB Act is less reliance on average. Schools have been able to hide the failure of certain groups of students in the past by the use of average learning. This is no longer possible; the learning of each subgroup must be reported. I am not defending the notion that a school should be labeled a failure if it doesn't meet adequate yearly progress in one of over 30 categories, but it is the right move to report results for the whole plus the various subgroups of students. We must "avoid using the average, or arithmetic mean, in understanding test scores."[21]

POOR STATISTICAL PRACTICE 11: ALPHABETICAL ORDER

Data for classrooms, like lists of stocks in the newspaper, are in alphabetical order. While this makes sense for easily finding data, it creates an overload when the need is to see the whole. Computers can take the alphabetical listing with subsequent numbers and create scatter diagrams. Figure 2.11 is a scatter diagram from the same set of five middle school math classrooms that have been shown before. The circle represents 10 students while the dot is one student. When the reader sees a dot inside the circle, it represents 11 students. What the scatter diagram shows is a dot for each student for each assessment, weekly in this case. The teacher and students can follow the movement from the lower left of the graph to the upper right. When the data are on a computer screen, it is possible to touch each cell of the scatter diagram to display the student names behind the dots.

While alphabetical order has some usefulness, at the same time it keeps the leaders from seeing a complete picture of the learning process.

CONTROL CHARTS ARE AN ALTERNATIVE TO RANKING

A chapter on poor statistics would be incomplete without introductory comments on control charts. They will be briefly explained later, but first there is a logical progression of thought necessary to understand their importance.

1. Statistics were developed to better understand variation.

2. Variation is always present.[22]

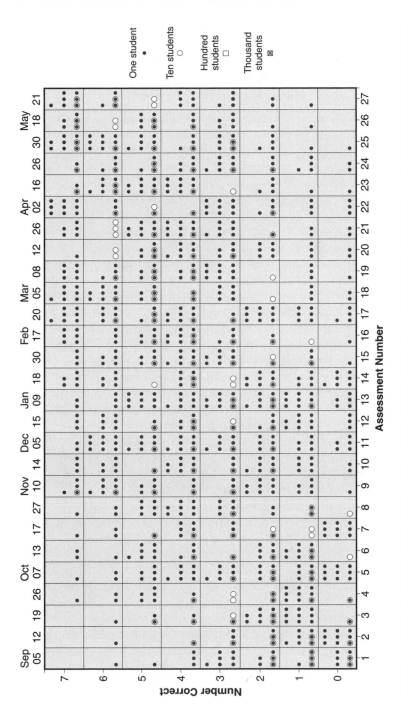

Figure 2.11 A scatter diagram of middle grade mathematics.

3. There are two kinds of variation: special and common.[23]

4. To properly deal with variation one must distinguish "assignable causes of variation" from "random elements."[24] Special variation is assignable and random variation is common.

In a fifth-grade classroom there may be students reading like the average fourth-, fifth-, or sixth-grade students. This is common variation. In the same classroom, however, there may be a student reading like an average first-grader and another reading like an average high school junior. Clearly this is special variation.

One of the difficulties with ranking is the assumption that first place is special-good and last place is special-bad. Nothing could be further from the truth. For example, if our fifth-grade classroom has students whose reading levels are spread out from 4.1 to 6.8, there is no special cause variation. Nobody is special in reading—neither the lowest nor the highest.

School administrators, equipped with control charts and test results can determine which classroom results (or schools) are common and which are special.[25] If the data show special-good, study to determine what can be replicated in other locales. For example, in one school district it was discovered that the cause of special-good in mathematics was skipping the first third of the textbook (review) and moving directly to the new content for that grade level. If the data are special-bad, determine the causes and remedy. For example, it was found in the same school district that the most common reason for special-bad was long-term substitute teachers. Administrators were providing assistance only with discipline.

I was intrigued to read the same insight in a well researched article by Pedro A. Noguera. When a principal was confronted with a problem, she indicated she knew about the problem but could do nothing about it until the regular teacher returned from maternity leave.[26]

Common variation does not mean good variation; it merely means that time must be spent improving the whole system and not studying individuals. In June of 2003, most U.S. newspapers carried articles about student writing. Most states and territories were ranked and the ensuing articles written. If the foundation for the articles had been a control chart (Figure 2.12), I suspect much more enlightened articles would have been written. The citizens of the United States would know (1) that Connecticut and Massachusetts have much to teach the rest of the states when it comes to writing, (2) that Guam and the Virgin Islands need immediate assistance, (3) the rest of the states are not much different from each other, and (4) writing is not a state-by-state problem, but a national issue.

Educators and journalists really do need a tool other than ranking. When educators rank other educators, as a principal did in Dallas, the

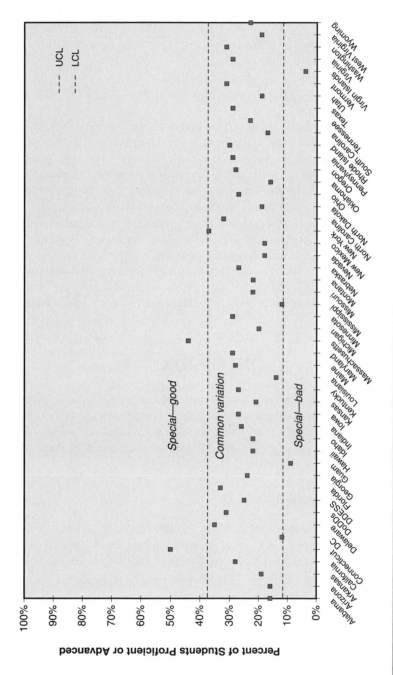

Figure 2.12 Control chart: national assessment of educational progress for grade 4 writing, 2003.

teachers complain.[27] When the journalists rank schools, the principals complain. In fact the heading of page two of a Minneapolis article was "Principals React Like Kids Getting Report Cards."[28] The control chart is the perfect solution to the ranking problem.

Ranking Psychology

The psychology behind ranking is 'educators in some states are lazy when it comes to writing instruction. Ranking will embarrass them so they will work harder and student writing will thus improve.' The psychology behind control charts is, 'the United States Department of Education has a responsibility to help all fifty states improve by (1) studying special-good for insight, (2) studying special-bad for ways to help, and (3) helping all other states with common variation to improve their writing systems for the good of the country.' What Deming wrote for managers could be rewritten for the U.S. Department of Education in regard to writing. "If management were to spend as much time and effort to improve processes as they do on ranking, rating, reward, and punishment for people at the top and the bottom, the results would be stupendous improvement in our economic position."[29]

CONCLUSION

Are Americans willing to adopt a new form of bragging? "I am so fortunate, my son was in a school last year where 100 percent of the seventh graders met the standards in all four core subjects." Or are we going to be content with bumper stickers that say, "My child is a winner; ha, ha, your child is left behind."

Key Recommendation

Use pretest data to display the L-shaped graph on the histogram. If the graph is already a bell curve prior to teaching, standards are too low. Monitor the bell-shaped curve during the year and put all instructional efforts into obtaining a J curve by year's end.

NO

Ranking

Bell curve

YES

Teamwork

J curve

3

The Pendulum

In the 1897 book *How to Teach Reading and What to Read in School,* G. Stanley Hall describes three approaches to reading: sentence, word, and sound. Since that time, America has recycled these three approaches over and over, each time announcing a new label. The sentence approach has been called literature-based, language experience, whole language, McGuffy,[1] and the Bible; the word method has been called sight, look-say, basal, and sometimes merely Dick and Jane. Since Dick and Jane there have been other attempts to bring back the word approach as in the 1972 story, "Home, Here We Come":

> "Look down here," said Quig. "I can see home! Can you see it, Zay?"
> "I can see it," said Zay. "Home! I can see it from here. Soon we will be home!"[2]

The sound approach has been labeled phonics, phonemic awareness, programmed, and direct instruction. In the 21st century, America still has only the same three approaches; none has been proven to be 100 percent effective.

ROOT CAUSE #3
The educational pendulum

This educational pendulum that moves from one focus to another and back again has not served American education well. Each time the pendulum swings, journalists describe the swing as subversive, maverick, or with some other eye-catching headline.[3] The pendulum is energized by researchers asking which of the three reading approaches is the best. Common sense tells us that when this question is asked, one of the approaches has to be in first place, one has to be in second place, and one is in third place. The problem is that none of the three approaches is 100 percent effective. The research questions should be, "How can all children learn to read?" "What schools have 100 percent literacy?" "What combinations of the three seem ideal?" "How much knowledge of the three approaches do teachers need in order to meet the learning needs of all students?"

The educational pendulum strikes each and every academic discipline. U.S. schools barely have their grammar, editing, parts-of-speech (information) program in place when the public becomes dissatisfied with writing (performance) instruction. So, education switches to a focus on writing. After five years of successful writing instruction, educators are aghast to pick up the newspapers and read how poorly children are performing on the standardized test of grammar. So, the politics heat up and soon the writing program is replaced with the new grammar program. It may even be that the superintendent who used so much energy to establish the exemplary writing system is replaced. Every subject in U.S. schools swings from focus on information to focus on performance back to focus on information, and so on.

Gunslingers have notches; educators have dents. The dents are on both sides of their heads. Why? They are continually being struck by pendulums.

If the reading pendulum plus the information/performance pendulum wasn't enough, there's a third pendulum. This swing says teach only reading and math. If schools triple the amount of time on reading and double the time on math, our students will be much more successful in life. So schools drop science, history, geography, music, art, and most physical education. But in a few years, some parents whose children learned to read in kindergarten and first grade set up a howl. This is not education, they clamor. So, the old curriculums are dusted off and all subjects are taught for another five years. That is, until educators are held accountable for only reading and math. They say, "I know that all subjects are important, but the political structure is set up to fire me if the reading and math scores don't go up."

It is no wonder that experienced teachers consider their classroom their hurricane shelter. Outside their classroom, three pendulums are clashing. The newly elected school board members have lassoed one pendulum, straddled it, and are waving their hats. The union, with no power to stop the pendulum, demands more salary to compensate for pendulum warfare stress. Ah, the bliss of the hurricane shelter.

Clearly, America will not have the schools it wants or deserves until the pendulums are stopped. We must understand what Michael Thompson wrote, "We must not be lured into a specious choice between excellent content and excellent process. (I don't have time for thinking skills, I have to cover the material! Or, We don't need to read books, we're training our brains to think for themselves!) It is a false dichotomy."[4]

So, how do educators and their political leaders stop the pendulum and start a life-long journey of continuous improvement? All three pendulums must be stopped. My suggestions are in no particular order.

ENERGY SOURCE FOR PENDULUMS

For each of the three pendulums, I have searched for the source of the energy that keeps them moving back and forth. Pendulums will stop if not provided more energy. The pendulum clock needs energy provided by the bobs in order to keep the hour and minute hands moving. If the weights are ignored, the pendulum stops and so does the clock. The educational pendulum never seems to stop: what is its energy source?

The energy source for the reading pendulum is the false belief that one of the three methods holds the key to 100 percent success in reading if educators just tried hard enough. When society accepts the fact that some children are confused and overwhelmed by the beauty of the complete sentences provided by music and literature and also accepts the fact that some children understand the whole of language and cannot ever remember which phonics rule to apply in particular situations, we will make great strides toward stopping the pendulum. We also must accept the fact that Dick and Jane and other programmed approaches work for some children. It is mind-boggling that our culture moved from children learning to read with sentences (Bible and McGuffy) to a belief that somehow learning to read with sentences (called whole language on the last pendulum swing) was evil. None of the three approaches are perfect and none are evil. Educators in both preservice and ongoing staff development need to learn from an expert who is passionate about one of the approaches and then another expert who is passionate about a second approach and finally an expert who is passionate about the third approach. Thus teachers, when faced with the daily needs of children, will draw on their knowledge of the three methods to assist all children in the learning to read process.

The energy source behind the teach-only-two-subjects pendulum is the belief that adjusting time is the only option available. It is amazing how highly some programs are touted that destroy all curriculum except reading and math. If one triples the time on reading and doubles the time on math, better results should occur. Big deal. If the time were tripled for music, think about how much music the next generation would know. Educators have the responsibility to instruct all children in all subjects and their political leaders must demand such. We do not have the right to rob a generation of the joy of learning any particular subject.

When the root causes described in this book are removed, students can meet grade-level expectations in reading and math and also have a balanced curriculum of all subjects. I'm not saying that in extreme remedial cases a student should not miss some instruction in a subject to garner extra help in Title I or special education; however, to make a schoolwide decision to triple reading and double math is flat-out wrong.

The energy source for the third pendulum is trivia. Requiring students to memorize trivia keeps the information/performance pendulum swinging. Here's how it works. During a time when the focus is on factual knowledge, students are memorizing trivia. After a while people are repulsed by this trivia and they say, "I hate facts; this can all be looked up on the Internet." So the focus changes completely to performance—no focus on spelling or grammar—only on writing. Well, the outcome of this complete switch is foreseeable. In five years, the cry reoccurs for factual knowledge and on goes the pendulum.

In order to stop this pendulum, educators have the responsibility to take trivia out of the required learning expectations. Every subject at every grade contains essential information that educated people should know. The National Research Council's clear recommendation is: "Have teachers make a distinction between those skills and processes students are to master versus those they are not."[5] Similarly, Douglas Reeves states, "a cardinal principle of quality: it is more important to measure a few things frequently than to measure a lot of things infrequently."[6] Every subject has trivia that can be taught, but students should not be graded on trivia knowledge. Providing students, for each and every course, the essential information to be placed in long-term memory is necessary to stop the pendulum. The combination of essential information plus performance expectations is the balance that can keep society from pointing out glaring deficiencies and fueling the pendulum.

Memorizing states and capitals is an example of trivia. Many students finish fifth grade knowing the states and capitals (the trivia), but don't know the essential. They may know that Santa Fe is the capital of New Mexico, but not have a clue where New Mexico is located. The essential geography information for fifth grade is knowing the location of the 50 states plus the location of major rivers, cities, mountains, and bodies of water. It is very important to know where New York City is located, but unnecessary for people in 49 states to know that the capital of New York is Albany. I realize that the difference between trivial and essential is a value judgment and reasonable people will disagree where to classify some content, but when educators are required to delineate the essential information for their courses they do agree in fairly short order.

Society will not allow educators to have a curriculum that is 100 percent performance. Society should not allow educators to have a curriculum that is 100 percent performance. Essential information is essential. The National Research Council described how experts differ from novices. Among other key principles they note, "Experts notice features and meaningful patterns of information that are not noticed by novices. Experts have acquired a great deal of content knowledge that is organized in ways that reflect a deep understanding of their subject matter."[7] The point is that experts are building on a foundation of information. These pendulum wars can be stopped by clearly stating essential information expectations and performance expectations for each course. Ideally the essential information is taught well, permission to forget is removed, and educators and their students can spend the majority of their time on performance because the essential information learning is documented.

A criticism of my work, as described in *Improving Student Learning,* is too much emphasis on factual knowledge. Critics say, "I don't care about facts—we're for higher order thinking skills in our district." What I hear from this comment is pendulum fuel, because the next person in charge will be for facts and the saga will go on and on. Michael Thompson wrote, "Thinking skills are essential, but we must apply these excellent thinking processes to excellent ideas. The content must be worthy of the effort."[8] Taking out the trivia not only provides a direction for factual knowledge, it gives time and purpose for the thinking skills.

If I had to choose between a student who knew grammar and a student who could write well, I'd select writing. If I had to choose between a student who could carry out meaningful science experiments and one who knew vocabulary and essential information, I'd choose the masterful science. Fortunately, I don't have to choose. When the requirement to learn trivia is removed from the schools, and permission to forget is stopped, there is ample time for competence in both information and performance.

The focus of this chapter is upon the instruction pendulum. However, other pendulums exist in education as well. Catherine Gewertz recently wrote about urban districts that are replacing their middle schools with K–8 schools. During my time as a school superintendent I changed two of our K–5 schools to K–8 schools and could write a complete article on the good that transpired from this adjustment. The 6–8 school and the K–8 schools all gained. Thus I was eager to read the article, but was soon disillusioned. Here's why. Referring to Philadelphia, she writes, "The district hopes that by 2008, the vast majority (of students) will attend K–8s."[9] Here is another pendulum in action. Districts can have both K–8 schools and middle schools. Both structures have advantages and disadvantages. Parents should be able to choose; it is not up to educators and their school boards to make these family choices either by eliminating all K–8 schools or all middle schools. In fact, I found that some families believed the K–8 was best for one of their children while the 6–8 was better for the sibling.

CONCLUSION

When students are being taught essential information, they are learning about important aspects of the past. Information is about the past. For example, in the past, people had many phonetic choices regarding how to spell words and they evolved into what we know today as correct spelling. All information learning is history. Mastering performance standards is about creating a better future for oneself and others. Every subject has performance expectations. Educators have many decisions to make, but the decision to focus only on the past information or on the performance expectations should not be available to them. All educators have responsibility for both. Likewise, educators must resist all pressure to offer only two subjects to elementary students and must not compromise student success based on whichever of the three reading approaches is in vogue at a particular time. The pendulums can, and must, be stopped.

Key Recommendation

Administrators and school board members should declare the pendulums dead in their school district. They should elicit everyone's help to root out all language that feeds any of these pendulums: reading methods, reading and math only, and information versus performance. Maybe the pendulum can actually be buried at a school board meeting.

NO
Information
or
performance

YES

Information
and
performance

4

Pressure versus Removing Barriers

A group of school superintendents are enjoying breakfast together when one of the members begins to complain about the governor. "The new requirements are certainly going to make things worse. Doesn't she understand that the more paperwork that is required, the less attention I pay to my community and the more attention I pay to the capitol?"

The meeting breaks up with no problems solved and the superintendents return to their local school districts. Some of the superintendents, certainly not all, send out directives, call meetings, give last-minute directions, and basically treat their principals exactly the way the governor is accused of treating the superintendents. The principals use their phone tree to invite all principals to the Friday watering hole ad-hoc meeting. The purpose of the meeting is to complain about the superintendent. What are we going to do about him?

The principals find themselves at the school on Saturday morning catching up on paperwork and getting ready for the new week. Some, certainly not all, place terse notes in the boxes of the teachers because of complaints last week. Any casual observer can see that some of the principals are treating their teachers exactly the way the superintendent is treating them.

The staff room is abuzz regarding the Monday morning "missiles" in their boxes. After a teacher is posted at the staff room door as a sentry, the conversation goes like this, "Doesn't he understand how discouraging it is to spend five hours over the weekend grading papers and preparing for this week, only to arrive in school to a negative directive?" The sad part is that some, certainly not all, of the teachers return to their classrooms and treat their students with the exact same poor behavior they witnessed in their principal.

Basically, it is difficult to manage others differently than one is being managed. We see the faults in our bosses, but not in ourselves. Basic to this domino leadership effect is that people tend to add pressure to those reporting to them rather than removing barriers. Deci wrote, "By failing to deal effectively with the stresses and pressures in their own lives, individuals add stresses and pressures to the lives of others." "Controlling others seems to be the sort of 'knee-jerk' reaction to feeling stress in any one-up position."[1]

ROOT CAUSE #4
Adding pressure versus removing barriers

THE SYSTEM IS THE PROBLEM

Deming wrote in *The New Economics* that 94 percent of the problems in any organization are caused by the system, and people cause six percent of the problems.[2] (He later raised the system estimate to 96 percent). If this theory is true, then most management decisions are flawed. Most teacher decisions are flawed. This book is about identifying the invisible barriers that are keeping people from doing their best. It is about describing the 94 percent to 96 percent of the problems that are caused by the system. The steps for wise use of this book are:

1. Internalize that almost all problems are caused by the system; not the people.

2. Study books such as this one that outline the deep, invisible system problems.

3. Study solutions, such as written by Marzano, Deci, Reeves, Senge, and Jenkins.

4. Continually remove barriers. For example, it is not nearly as important to adopt a new program as it is to remove permission to forget what is already taught in the current program. It is not nearly as important to have an inservice day as it is to remove ranking practices that are discouraging a majority of the students.

Examples abound in the literature regarding the intense amount of pressure added to educators. Here are three examples:

1. "Imagine you are a teacher in an inner-city elementary school. You are dedicated to providing your students with a rigorous academic education, and to creating a caring and stable environment. Today you arrive early, as usual, to review student work and prepare the day's lessons. As you walk into your classroom, you find it totally rearranged: All of your students' work has been taken down from the walls, the desks are rearranged, and new, ready-made posters have been put up to replace the student work. This is not a case of vandalism, you discover. The principal has commissioned another teacher to 'fix' your classroom by putting the furniture in proper order and making more room for positing school rules and motivational slogans."[3]

2. "Districts were (in the words of teachers) long on pressure and short on support with the predictable effect that much of the learning that did occur around ambitious instructional practice was idiosyncratic by school and classroom."[4]

3. "Some school staffs expressed a willingness to use findings generated from the research to modify their reform plans. At the most troubled schools, however, administrators were more likely to claim that they could not use the information because they were under too much pressure."[5]

CONSEQUENCES OF ALL THIS PRESSURE

"University of Pennsylvania researcher Richard M. Ingersoll has debunked the idea that retirement is creating a crisis in the availability of teachers. In truth, fewer people retire each year than leave teaching because of dissatisfaction with schools and school districts as workplaces. The problem is not a lack of people qualified to be teachers, but a shortage of people willing to work under the human-resources conditions that prevail in school districts."[6]

"The conventional wisdom is that we can't find enough good teachers. The truth is that we can't keep enough good teachers."[7] Of course, not all teachers respond to the pressure by leaving education. Most respond by adding more pressure to the lives of their students and some even respond by adding pressure to parents. Lebanon, Pennsylvania, for example, explored the idea "that parents be graded on how involved they are in their children's education."[8]

For the people who remain in education, Senge and Deci describe what happens. Senge writes, "Hierarchical authority, as it has been used traditionally in Western management, tends to evoke compliance, not foster results. The more strongly hierarchical power is wielded, the more compliance results."[9] Deci states, "In this condition (of continual pressure) people can reasonably be described as alienated." They also have the urge to defy. This urge comes with compliance.[10]

Another result of the pressure is distorted figures. One does not have to read the news for very long to find instances of student distorting (cheating), educator distorting (manipulating test scores), business distorting (Enron), and government agency distortion of the facts.

Even more discouraging is the fact that all the pressure does no good in the long term. "Fear can produce extraordinary changes in short periods,"[11] but education is, at the minimum, a thirteen-year endeavor from kindergarten to grade 12. Deci wrote, "Richard Ryan and I frequently talk to teachers and parents about motivation. Teachers tell us about parents who haven't done a good job of parenting, and parents complain about teachers."[12] Teachers who are pressuring students, and parents who respond by pressuring teachers, are not bringing about the desired result of long-term improvement. Fear and pressure are failed management strategies.

WHO IS RESPONSIBLE FOR BARRIER REMOVAL?

"It is the responsibility of management to discover the barriers that prevent workers from taking pride in the work they do."[13] It is well understood that the manager of the school is the principal and the manager of the school district is the superintendent. Mary Walton's quote of Deming applies to all levels of management, however. This includes the managers of the classroom (teachers) and the manager of the state (governor).

Leaders have the power to remove barriers; students and employees do not have this power. The problem is that leaders don't know what the barriers are. How can they determine what the barriers are? Ask the people "below" them in the organization. Teachers ask pupils, principals ask teachers, superintendents ask principals, and governors ask superintendents. I'm not saying governors don't need to listen to everyone, but this is certainly a place to start.

SUGGESTIONS FOR BARRIER REMOVAL

"Consider developing a systematic way for your school district to pursue 'organized abandonment' or eliminating unnecessary practices. Educators are better at piling things higher and deeper (especially on teachers) and not particularly good at learning to get rid of what doesn't work, what isn't needed, or what gets in the way of the main job of teaching students."[14]

What follows in this chapter are suggestions for barrier removal. All are systematic and require people to agree that taking items "off the plate" is a top priority. Certainly this list is not complete; there are other possibilities, but once students know the teacher is serious about removing barriers and once the teachers know the principal is serious, ideas will abound.

Barrier Removal Suggestion 1: Structured Listening

The opposite of control is being able to take the other person's perspective and work from there.[15] The only way to take another perspective is listening and the open-door policy won't accomplish this goal. Listening skill is on a continuum from (1) I listen to my friends to (2) open door to (3) formal, regular listening to the group. Many teachers will drop everything to listen to a student who requests to speak with them after school. It is rare, however, for a teacher to ask monthly, "What went well this month and what could I do to make next month better?" This is level-three listening—formal and consistent. When such formal listening is the norm, people will feel much more a part of the organization.

Teachers would love a poster in the staff room entitled, "Barriers keeping us from doing our best." Staff are invited to list barriers—not gripes—to doing their best. It is then up to principals to remove as many barriers as possible and acknowledge the ones that they cannot remove.

Principals desire the same opportunity. What are the barriers the superintendent and school board can remove? And think of the joy that could be created in a state with a governor asking educators to list the barriers, most written into current law, that could be legislatively removed. No Child Left Behind provides a perfect opportunity. The governor can easily state, "The federal government has added great pressure to your lives. I know all of you want your schools to be successful and meet the rising expectations. What laws and regulations are currently wasting a significant amount of your time and money that could be dropped so that you can concentrate on having more students meet the standards for their grade level?"

"They used to call me 'the prosecutor,' because I would hone in on a question," said Wurtzel (CEO of Circuit City). "You know, like a bulldog, I wouldn't let go until I understood. Why, why, why?"[16] Governors need this same bulldog attitude. Why do we have this education law? Why? Why? Why?

Barrier Removal Suggestion 2: Use Formal Power Appropriately

People will not speak openly when they fear that power will be abused. Deming provided for us the three sources of power for a leader. Remember, these sources apply to the teacher as well as the governor and administrator. The three sources are formal, personality, and knowledge.[17] The most effective leaders rely mostly on knowledge, then personality, and rarely upon formal power. If the leader is consumed with making sure that everyone knows who is in charge, then power is the dominate asset and listening will be stunted.

Barrier Removal Suggestion 3: Remove Barriers Between Staffs

"Canadian Airlines . . . had long encouraged its flight attendants to refer to the business-class passengers by name. There was a slight problem however. The manifest printed only the first six characters of the passengers' last names."[18] This seems like such a simple example of one department not speaking with another department. Educators are daily frustrated with such examples: The purchasing department, whose job is to save money, obtains a great price on construction paper. The paper is never ordered from the district warehouse by teachers, however, because it is not the right shade of red for either Christmas or Valentine's Day.

The biggest barrier is between elementary, middle, and high school teachers. Principals see each other regularly at meetings, but teachers rarely see each other and don't work together on common goals. The first step in removing these barriers is to publicly admit they exist. List them on a chart in the staff room. The barriers can only be removed one at a time and only if they are known by people who can do something about each of them. If there is a barrier between purchasing and the needs of teachers, then bring together the interested parties. Change occurs "primarily as a consequence of interaction."[19]

Barrier Removal Suggestion 4: Have Meaningful Answers

When students ask, "Why do I need to learn this?", have a meaningful answer or search it out. "Our main complaint as students (and this has not changed) was not that the work was too hard, but that it was boring, and this complaint was and still is valid. 'Boring' usually meant that we could not relate what we were asked to do with how we might use it in our lives . . . it is almost impossible for bored workers to do high-quality work."[20]

Barrier Removal Suggestion 5: Use Appraisal to Listen

"An appraisal process . . . should recognize that people have a right to take joy in their work and it should help them to increase that joy; it should recognize that people also strive to be a part of a team and it should help them to increase that sense of joy in family; and it should aim to develop and continuously improve people by assisting the leader in the improvement of the process."[21] Most teachers would agree with this process when studying how their principal evaluates them. The question is, however, do they agree with the statement when they are evaluating students?

Barrier Removal Suggestion 6: Pursue a Common Goal

Forget the false belief that best efforts will improve your organization. When everybody is doing their best, we often have chaos, with each person's individual goals undermining the goals of others. People working together pursuing a common aim is the alternative.

Barrier Removal Suggestion 7: Deal with Lack of Time Issues

Warren Bennis wrote, "I had become the victim of a vast, amorphous, unwitting, unconscious conspiracy to prevent me from doing anything whatever to change the university's status quo. Even those of my associates who fully shared my hopes to set new goals, new directions, and to work toward creative change were unconsciously often doing the most to make sure I would never find the time to begin." He then captured the essence of the problem: "Bennis's First Law of Academic Pseudodynamics: Routine work drives out nonroutine work and smothers to death all creative planning, all fundamental change in the university—or any institution."[22] Douglas Reeves reminds us, "Before any new initiative, the leader is obliged to consider the fixed number of hours in the school day. Because creating and evaluating performance assessment is so time-consuming, the leader cannot add it as a new initiative. First he must identify some units, activities, chapters, or curriculum that can be terminated."[23]

The quality everyone desires depends heavily upon barrier removal, and none of the barriers seems so overwhelming as the lack of time. Those not involved in education have no concept of the number of 14-hour days and the number of summer, unpaid requirements. So, how do we overcome this time barrier? I suggest that school staffs list the ways they spend their time and then classify them under the headings of features and quality.

Myron Tribus helped me understand the difference. A car that has quality starts when the key is turned in the ignition, stops when the brakes are applied, steers correctly, and generally can be depended on—it always works. A feature is a nice extra such as a button for driver 1 and a button for driver 2. When driver 1 enters the car, she pushes the button and all mirrors and the driver's seat adjust to her specifications. The second button does the same for driver 2. This nice button is a feature and is worthless if the car won't start.

Quality, as stated earlier, means that the public can depend on its schools. Quality will not occur as long as schools spend so much time on features, such as designated weeks for a particular focus, that have no relationship to classroom instruction, and activities and projects that meet the need of outside agencies, not the students. For example, participating in a Christmas tree decoration contest at the local department store is an unnecessary feature. The store gets its decorations for free, parents come into the store to see their children's decorations, the business wins, and the students lose. There are hundreds of features in schools. If quality was in place, I'd applaud all of them, but when quality is not consistent, the features must be removed to provide time for improvement. Quality will not occur without time for educators to meet together to create this quality. Dropping many features will go a long way toward creating this time.

State leaders have been removing the significant barrier of too much responsibility upon the individual teacher. Teachers had the responsibility for almost everything and thus the efforts were uncoordinated. The following is a past, current, and future look at responsibilities.

Responsibility	Past	Current	Future
Standards	Teacher	State	State
Assessment	Teacher	State	State and district
Curriculum	School district	School district	School and district
Instruction	Teacher	Teacher	Teacher and teacher teams

I recognize that this view cannot match all 50 states and all school districts, but it is a close approximation of what has occurred and needs to take place. Clearly it was too much responsibility for each teacher to determine standards and assessments (by default the textbook publishers took on this job.) A committee of educators and public representatives is the appropriate body to determine standards and assessments. Curriculum has been too tightly controlled by school districts in many places. There are places where the control is necessary, which novels are going to be used at each grade level, for example. But there are many other places where the focus from the school district needs to be on students meeting state standards with less concern about which approach is used by particular schools. More teachers working in teams is also a great need because the strengths of individual teachers can be realized by more students.

The ideal is for departments and grade levels to have weekly or biweekly data on the learning of their department or their grade level and for staffs to plan together how they will increase learning. It is not a competitive set of data comparing one classroom to another, but a cooperative set of data whereby all teachers are doing their best to have all students meet high standards.

Barrier Removal Suggestion 8: Help Parents; Don't Pressure Them

"One study of four federal education programs found that the most frequently used school-to-home communication mechanisms were newsletters, bulletins, and flyers, all of which provide little opportunity for parents to respond."[24] "Fan and Chen focus on the manner and extent to which parents communicate their academic aspirations to their children. The relationship between this dynamic and student achievement is fairly straightforward—high expectations communicated to students are associated with enhanced achievement," writes Marzano. He further states that "the most important aspect of socioeconomic status (SES) is the effect of the home environment, as opposed to factors such as parental income and education. Where a child cannot change the income, education, or occupation of adults in the home, it can have a potential impact on the atmosphere in the home."[25]

Barrier Removal Suggestion 9: Classify Knowledge in the Most Logical Format

"Teachers must structure content in such a way as to highlight its 'sameness.' "[26] Appendix C is a listing of essential concepts as Jeff Burgard provided for his eighth-grade science classroom.[27] The classification is an assistance in the learning of the concepts.

Barrier Removal Suggestion 10: Interdisciplinary Time Savers

"The criterion of leverage helps the leader and teachers identify those standards applicable to many academic disciplines. Two examples that one can find in every set of academic standards are nonfiction writing and interpretation of tables, charts, and graphs."[28] Science and math teachers do not both need to teach metric measurement; both can assess, but only one department need teach metric measurement.

Barrier Removal Suggestion 11: Study Discipline Practices

The barrier is that students must cooperate and get along with all of their teachers in order to be successful in any of their classes. If a student swears at a teacher and is sent to the office, the typical punishment is suspension from school for a period of time. To further complicate matters, some schools have a policy that students must receive zeros in all assignments missed because of suspension. So the student is now behind in all classes, not only the one where he swore at the teacher. A barrier needs to be removed. The high school could suspend the student from only the class where he/she swore. The student could then report to the office for the two to three day period of the punishment during that class period only. I am not minimizing the swearing, but am saying that sometimes our rules establish barriers that keep students from achieving the education we are paid to provide.

Barrier Removal Suggestion 12: Do Policies Interfere with Student Success?

Study all policies that may interfere with the aim of all students being successful. For example, a significant barrier to learning to read, for some children, is continuous head lice. Every time lice are discovered, these children are sent home. Sometimes, just by following the rules, school staff send home students from 25 to 50 days of a school year. By the time the children are old enough to help solve this problem on their own, the optimal learning-to-read window is over. Remove this barrier by assisting the children in school and letting them return to their learning. The normal response is to apply pressure on the family. It doesn't work.

Revise homework policies and practices to remove barriers. For example, when homework is not being turned in at an acceptable rate, teachers can either proceed to explain the bad things that are going to happen (pressure) if students don't do their homework or teachers can ask students how the process can be changed to help students be more successful with the homework assignments (removing barriers). When teachers ask, "What can I do to help you do more homework?" it is amazing what great suggestions are given. Is the homework completion rate now 100 percent? No, but it has increased.

CONCLUSION

Barrier removal is a necessary step in the process of providing quality education. What is quality? For schools, quality means happy students meeting both essential information and performance standards. This quality can be depended on from class to class and grade level to grade level. Currently, both educators and the public know that quality cannot be depended on in today's public and private schools. Very active parents can navigate a course through schools to provide quality for their children, but the school districts do not provide a system where students are consistently happy and consistently meeting educational standards.

Key Recommendation

Remove two barriers for every one new initiative; remove two education laws for every one new law.

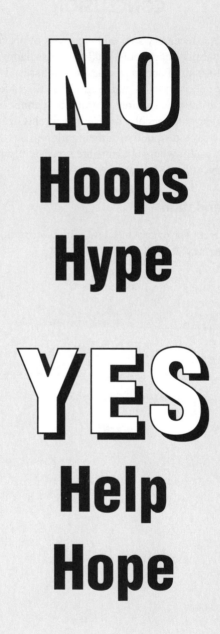

Source: John Maxwell, *The Maxwell Leadership Bible,* Thomas Nelson Publishers, Nashville, TN, 2002, p. 1131.

5

Change after Change with No Improvement

Imagine a small child on a rocking horse; the joy seems to increase as the movement accelerates. The change is constant; up and down, down and up goes the horse and its rider. Mom steps away for a minute to start dinner, comes back to check on the youngster, and makes two observations: the rider and horse are in the exact same position they were at the last observation yet the change is continual. Many educators would describe themselves as the child on the rocking horse. The change is continual, but forward momentum is lacking.

The process is easy to describe. Somebody with influence attends a conference, picks up a good idea, convinces others of the merit of the idea, and a change is born. Unintentionally a fight is also born; it starts in six months with 49 percent of the people saying this change made things worse and 51 percent saying it made things better.

ROOT CAUSE #5
Making change after change, with no improvement

FLAVOR OF THE MONTH

Most corporations have had so many "flavor-of-the-month" initiatives from management that people immediately discount any new pronouncement as more "executive cheerleading."[1] Educators can take some consolation from Senge's observation of business and know that they are not alone; business is plagued with the same disease. Further, even more evidence is provided that achieving more businesslike practices is not education's savior.

From their business observations, Deming and one of his students, William Scherkenbach, made similar statements. Scherkenbach wrote, "Reorganization is easy and vitally necessary, but it is no panacea for improvement."[2] Deming stated, "Ninety-five per cent of changes made by management today make no improvements."[3] It might be wise to have veteran teachers agree on the five percent of the changes made in their career that actually improved student learning.

One of the reasons that both business and education adopt new ideas regularly is the pressure. Jim Collins wrote, "People who say, 'Hey, but we've got constraints that prevent us from taking this longer-term approach,' should keep in mind that the good-to-great companies followed this model no matter how dire the short-term circumstances." Collins implores us to understand that all organizations feel the pressure to make improvements *right now,* but that the great companies resist the pressure to make changes that are only good for the short-term. Being able to resist the pressure for *right now* improvements seem to be one of the most necessary ingredients to stopping the change-but-no-improvement rocking horse. Collins further writes, "Kroger, like all good-to-great companies, developed its ideas by paying attention to the data right in front of it, not by following trends and fads set by others."[4]

Noguera wrote, "Clearly many of the schools hoped to raise test scores without actually improving instruction or aligning the curriculum with the standards. Recognizing that efforts to improve the quality of teaching would take years to bear fruit, the schools commonly respond to high-stakes testing by teaching test-taking skills to students who were behind academically. This strategy was clearly ineffective."[5]

After years of change after change after change many educators have become bitter. So much energy was used up on the series of changes. This is compounded by the fact that education has so many bosses—state legislators, the governor, the state superintendent, college entrance test publishers, federal legislators, the Office of Civil Rights, the local school board, and so on. Each of these agencies feel it is their duty to bring about their version of a change. And the reason many of these people aspired to their current leadership position is they despised the direction of their predecessor's changes. Each time new school board members or new anybody come on board, people brace for a fight.

EVIDENCE OF CHANGE WITH NO IMPROVEMENT

"In the past decade, more than half of Kentucky's public high schools have abandoned traditional 45-minute classes for longer periods aimed at improving student achievement. But a new study by Murray State University has found that schools that have adopted longer classes—known as block scheduling—score approximately the same on state standardized tests as schools with traditional schedules."[6]

"In recent decades, the vast majority of states began requiring applicants for teaching jobs in public schools to pass statewide certification exams. The idea was to raise teacher quality by ensuring that they met minimum standards for basic skills and subject knowledge." Unfortunately, teacher testing doesn't seem to have achieved that goal, report Joshua Angrist and Jonathan Guryan in a recent National Bureau of Economic Research working paper. They went on to report that teacher testing raised teacher salaries, but found no evidence it raised the quality of new teachers.[7]

Phillip Schlechty observes, "Changes in schools are the result of changes in the larger society, not educational changes. In spite of all the change, not much is really different."[8] Richard Elmore makes the same observation, writing, "this situation (in public schools) produces lots of change and not much improvement."[9] The problem is everywhere, even in Arizona. "The state has no information whether programs work or not."[10] Millions of dollars are often spent on new programs without collecting the required baseline data. And when it is collected, a government agency often changes the exam so there is no valid post-exam.

EVIDENCE OF CHANGE WITH IMPROVEMENTS

Russell M. Gersten, an education professor at the University of Oregon, said that his own review of studies in mathematics turned up only two practices that boost student achievement—peer tutoring and giving students regular feedback on their progress.[11] Gersten's research documents that some changes lead to improvement. Not all changes are a waste of time.

How to Know If a Change Results in Improvement

The reason people have two little fingers is to place one in each ear when the "idea of the century" comes along. Preparation can begin when the boss leaves for the conference. Nobody will listen to the new ideas from the conference unless "the motto is, no more changes *until* there is a plan whereby everyone can know if the change results in improvement."

How does the change agent convince colleagues to remove their pinkies from their ears? The answer is to establish, in the planning process, a method of determining when the changes result in improvement. It is not necessary that all of the staff members of a school agree on the merits of a change, but it is essential that at least 90 percent agree on the method of studying the change. People can disagree on the merits of a proposed new student discipline plan, but must agree how they will know if the change is an improvement. For example, a staff could agree that after two years of implementation, if it cannot be proved that fewer students are in the office for discipline infractions, then the new plan sunsets and the school reverts to the former system.

In summary, here's the history and proposed sequence of thought that needs to take place in schools:

Schools, like business, have followed the flavor of the year.

The continual changes have not improved education.

Staff members have become very tired of the changes. Teachers can behave like saints when in their classrooms with their students and like the devil himself when in a staff meeting discussing a change.

Status quo is ensured because there are always people willing to try the new change and there are always resisters. Status quo is not an absence of activity, but a balance of power. In the U.S. Senate we call it *gridlock.*

However, the new thought process, with a new history should be:

Agree that improvement is needed.

Agree that without change, no improvement is possible.

Agree that before any change is instituted, an agreement will be reached regarding how to assess if the change actually resulted in improvement.

Agree that if no improvement results in an agreed upon time, the change will go away.

Agree that if improvement does result from the change, the new change will be cemented into the fabric of the school's normal operating procedures.

THE FEDERAL GOVERNMENT'S ATTEMPT TO HELP

Maybe the federal government is attempting to stop this education rocking horse by mandating that schools only implement scientifically researched and proven methodology. If all educational knowledge in the world were known, this would be a good idea. A better law would be to either implement proven methods or a scientific process to study the proposed change. And the process should be applied to all changes, including purchasing a new textbook. The legislature should live by the same rules. If a new law does not bring about improvement in three to five years, it automatically goes away. The same should be true for school board policy.

THREE TO FIVE WEEKS

One of the aspects of the process described in my book *Improving Student Learning* that excites me the most is that a teacher, or a group of teachers, can implement a new strategy and know in three to five weeks if the change results in improvement. The students see the teachers as learning scientists. They openly share their hypotheses with the students and all together they study the results. This works with kindergartners learning their letters, sounds, and sight words all the way up to graduate courses. Tribus is writing about his work with Feurenstein when he states, "The teacher and the student are together, evaluating the learner's learning process. They are seeking ways to improve it."[12] This is the essence of making changes and studying them to see if they result in improvement.

ADOPT NEW LANGUAGE

My advice to teachers is to listen to administrator proposals with an open mind, lead the effort to change the language from "new plan" to "current hypothesis," and assist in the testing of the hypotheses.

It is crucial for our egos to revise our language from *plans* to *hypotheses*. When *plan* is used, our ego is attached to the outcome. We really do want the plan to be popular. When *hypothesis* is used, egos can be set aside while studying the data. We can even say, in spite of the fact that a particular system worked elsewhere, it has not proven successful here.

BE SURE TO MEASURE THE ULTIMATE GOAL

When studying change one must be very sure an adequate measure is chosen. The measure must be of the ultimate goal, not a subset of the goal. For example, a school could implement a new phonics program and show great increases in student knowledge of phonics. The problem is that phonics is not the goal; reading is the goal. Reading should be measured. Are students better readers? That's the question to be answered to determine if the change resulted in improvement. The same could be said for plans to increase homework completion rates. The measure is not homework, but learning the content or meeting performance standards is the aim. Did students learn more science because we increased the science homework completion rate? That is the improvement we are after.

I cannot help but give another example. A principal promises students that if they read 25,000 books, he will shave off his beard and eat it. The kids love it, they read (or at least report reading), parents sign documents, teachers collect data, and the media covers the event, but there is not one shred of evidence documented that reading ability actually increases. We must measure what we really desire in order to determine if the changes result in improvement.

Conyers and Ewy write similarly, when they describe their first change that made a real difference in school improvement. It was to measure performance, not implementation of something. They state, "The assumption was that if the program or practice improvements were implemented, student performance would improve. While this may seem a reasonable assumption, district test scores usually firmly refuted the assumption."[13]

SYSTEM IMPROVEMENT OVER TIME

According to Richard Elmore, "Improvement . . . is change with direction, sustained over time, that moves entire systems, raising the average level of quality and performance while at the same time decreasing the variation among units."[14] As I write this I can't help but recall a California worry. When Governor Wilson and the legislature provided funds to reduce class size in grades K–3 from over 30 to 20, I supported the decision and implemented this reduction. The testimonials were great from teachers regarding the improved learning. My worry was, did the system capture the improvement? If it is true that with smaller classes teachers could accomplish in eight months what used to take 10 months and then have two more months of additional learning, what happens to this gain if the next year's teacher starts in August at the exact same place in the curriculum? It seems the system may not have been able to move as a whole, even though parts are excelling. Teachers, particularly those from California, should not read this as a suggestion to return to the horrible class sizes of the past, but consider the need to couple the efforts of all primary teachers so than an extra year of learning can take place in kindergarten through grade three. Elmore has set a high standard for what improvement is. And Deming reminds us that leaders have an obligation to use formal power to bring improvement to the system—equipment, materials, and methods.[15]

CONTINUAL IMPROVEMENT

Another problem with programs and change is they communicate that once something is implemented, we are done. Actually, we are never done. If a school cuts its discipline referrals down from 500 per year to 175, it first wants to secure the gains and then start over and reduce even further. It is simple to write such a statement, but most difficult to implement. My conversations with assistant principals tell me they are so busy dealing with problems, they have no time to even think about how to make the system better. Mistake. "The manager's own workday must be organized to give productivity improvement, through improvement of the system, a high priority. If the manager is not so committed and does not organize his or her working time, the job will not be done. It is the one essential job of the manager's job that cannot be delegated."[16] Deming recognized that managers "must of course solve problems and stamp out fires as they occur, but these activities do not change the system."[17] Full-time counseling and punishing does not change the system. A full-time assistant principal dealing with discipline problems adds no more to a school than a full-time mechanic fixing warranty repairs. If the assistant principal is now only spending a quarter of his or her time on discipline, however, the school has the asset of a new three-quarter person that actually can add value to learning.

CONCLUSION

Educators must stop flitting from change to change. Instead they need to become so burdened over the needs that they are willing to go slow to go fast.

Going slow means no change until it is agreed how the change will be evaluated to know if anything actually improved. *Going fast* means significantly reducing the number of changes so there is a chance of maintaining the few changes that actually result in improvement.

Key Recommendation

Make no changes until affected people agree how all will know if the change actually results in improvement. Speak of hypotheses much more and plans far less.

NO
Change
More change

YES
Improvement
More improvement

6

The False Belief
That Experience Is the
Best Teacher

I often ask seminar participants to rank how people learn best: mentoring, experience, or testing theories. The responses typically are that 85 percent of the people believe experience is the best teacher, 10 percent state that mentoring is best, and only five percent state that testing theories is the best way to learn. Not only this, but our folklore keeps saying experience is the best teacher, as was printed on an anonymous list of "wisdom" recently circulated to me. It displayed "the most destructive habit" as "worry," "the greatest asset" as "faith," and, of course, "our greatest teacher" is "experience." It is thus an uphill battle to convince people that testing theories is the number one way to learn.

EXPERIENCE IS A TEACHER, JUST NOT THE BEST TEACHER

I will not argue that experience never teaches. Experience does teach and Dale Carnegie was correct when he wrote in 1936 about experience as a teacher. He wrote, "By myself, I opened my engagement book . . . and asked myself: What mistakes did I make this time? What did I do that was right—and in what way could I have improved my performance? What lessons can I learn from that experience?"[1] My argument is that education will be able to make great strides when it ranks learning methods as (1) learn from testing theories, (2) learn from mentors, and (3) learn from experience.

EDUCATIONAL RESEARCH

Educational research often does not have a positive impact on educators' professional lives. It seems research is available to support about any point of view. Educators can quickly discount research and live by their experience. Hopefully, work such as *What Works in Schools,* written by Bob Marzano, will reverse this situation. Much can be learned by synthesis of the research.

It is completely understandable why the majority of educators don't believe that testing theories is the best way to learn. Their experience has not been positive in regard to research. And even if they have a positive outlook toward research, they think research is done by somebody else, not them. They are too busy.

The simple concepts of this chapter, however, when implemented, will document for teachers that continual testing of theories is possible. Then and only then will educators no longer accept that experience is the best teacher.

ROOT CAUSE #6
The false belief that experience is the best teacher

TESTING THEORY EXAMPLE

For purposes of illustration, I will return to the assistant principal's role in taking care of discipline. The job is not to discipline whomever is sent into the office. The responsibility is to increase the number of students with one or zero referrals and reduce the number of students who have many referrals. The overall aim is to make the school a safer place because students are behaving better.

When assistant principals internalize the belief that they are to improve the whole discipline system, they must have a method of easily testing out theories. The first step is to establish a process for collecting and communicating the data. Each Friday, prior to leaving for the weekend, these assistant principals post on a bulletin board in the hallway the number of discipline referrals for the past week. There are no names, only a series of weekly totals. Everyone can see how last week went compared to every other week. If assistant principals merely add graphing to their hectic

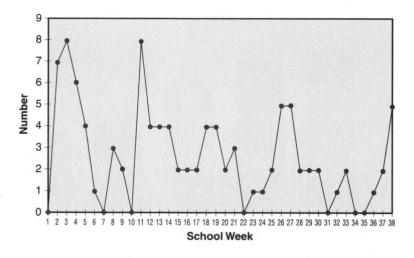

Figure 6.1 Trend of discipline referrals—PI Middle School 2003–04.

schedule, nothing improves though they have a little more experience counting and graphing. Figure 6.1 is an actual example of such a graph from Darren Overton, Pine Island, Minnesota, middle school principal.

The job is not to count and graph, but to always be choosing hypotheses to test in order to lower the number of weekly referrals. If staff state the problem is full moons, then have science students plot the phases of the moon over the discipline graph to see if the hypothesis is correct. If it is correct, then the assistant principal is to lead the planning to see if future full moons can be normal days and not days with many referrals. If the moon is not the culprit, then other hypotheses need to be brainstormed and researched. The responsibility of the people in charge of behavior is to continually study ideas to make the school safer. Some of these ideas will come from students and others from adults. All can be researched in a simple fashion. Figure 6.2, also from Pine Island, shows the results of five years of this process applied to student discipline.

PLAN–DO–STUDY–ACT

Deming named this process plan–do–study–act (PDSA). By *plan,* he meant the establishment of baseline data, disaggregation of data, and brainstorming of solutions. The assistant principal's chart on the wall of weekly referrals is the baseline data. Such a simple task as counting and plotting gives

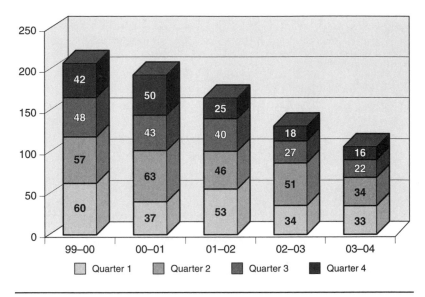

Figure 6.2   Total Pine Island Middle School discipline referrals 1999–2004.

the foundation for testing out theories on improved behavior. The second aspect of planning is having disaggregated data. This can be classifying discipline referrals by gender, ethnicity, time of day, day of the week, phase of the moon, wind, temperature, or type of infraction. Such looks at the data by category will generate hypotheses for testing. The third aspect of planning is what one would assume—generate a plan. The *do* is simply testing out the theory. The *study* is as it sounds—study the results. Did the new plan cause students to behave better or not? The *act* has two aspects. The first is to cement any improvement into the organization so it is not lost, and the second is to start over with PDSA.

"What does improve instruction and raise levels of achievement? A team of teachers meeting regularly—and continuously—to design, test, and then adjust their lessons and strategies in light of results."[2] Deming's PDSA can guide this advice for regular teacher meetings.

"I love to visualize charts, so much so that my staff would jokingly call me 'Chart Boy' when they thought I wasn't listening."[3] This quote from Guilani highlights the importance of charts and graphs in the study phase. Tables of data do not communicate nearly as well as simple graphs. I would say that study without the use of graphs is useless. Think about a teacher with 120 high school students and 20 entries for each student. Too many numbers are present to visualize what is happening.

What happens in school far too often is the opposite of PDSA. John Merrow wrote about this for *USA Today.* " 'If you can provide kids with extra time,' said school board member Terri Thomson of summer school, 'they improve.' " "Actually," wrote Merrow, "I don't think the kind of 'extra time' now offered matters a bit. Summer school, in New York and elsewhere, is little more than mindless repetition of failed practices. Yet summer school is being mandated in a growing number of public systems around the country."[4]

Ironically, from New York City itself comes a great description of PDSA without using the terms Deming used. Giuliani writes, "Don't announce an initiative until the results are already in. Try it out, refine it, get at least a preliminary set of results—then announce the plan. It's much like the production of a play. When possible, producers don't launch a new show directly on Broadway. They start it in another city, where it'll attract less scrutiny, and tinker with it for awhile before the stakes grow too high."[5]

The summer school plan is sorely lacking the elements of PDSA. It has a third of the plan, the do, no study, and no act. I'm not writing this to disparage decision makers in New York City, but to describe what is typical. We get an idea and go for it as if the idea were truth. It is not truth. Peter Senge states this so well, "Reflective openness starts with the willingness to challenge our own thinking, to recognize that any certainty we ever have is, at best, a hypothesis about the world. No matter how compelling it may be, no matter how fond we are of 'our idea' it is always subject to test and improvement."[6]

A very encouraging article about schools testing theories comes from Detroit. Janet Sugameli reports the results of an experiment with a night school for high school students. The school meets from 4 PM to 10 PM four days a week. The school has data on improved attendance and improved graduation rates.[7] Schools can test out their hypotheses.

STATISTICS FOR MASTER'S DEGREES

One of the major reasons educators are not regularly testing hypotheses is a lack of knowledge regarding exactly how to proceed. The statistics course in master's degree programs is often the wrong course. (Many universities realize it is the wrong course, so they eliminate statistics. Wrong decision.) Students working on their master's degrees and those studying for their doctorates are often in the same course. The course is entirely appropriate for doctoral students preparing to write a research dissertation. It is not the course needed by master's students, however. In their book *Charting Your*

Course, Conyers and Ewy, who led Community Consolidated School District 15 to earn the Malcolm Baldrige National Quality Award in 2003, list the tools that should be learned in the replacement master's statistics course.[8] Susan Leddick and others describe all the necessary details of each of the statistical tools in *Total Quality Tools for Education (K–12).*[9]

The simplest method for educators to use to test hypotheses is with the baseline data for one hypothesis at a time. The assistant principal with the graph for the weekly discipline referrals is an example. When multiple hypotheses need to be tested, design of experiments (DOE) works exceedingly well. DOE would work well, for example, in the New York City summer school example. The school board and educators have multiple hypotheses regarding what will work best for the students. Instead of seeing which hypothesis can garner the most board member votes, DOE could be used to test out several hypotheses at once.

DOE IN THE CLASSROOM

DOE is an easy methodology for educators to test out various methods and theories. Many variations exist for DOE; all are based on the number of hypotheses. I've listed the necessary structure (in Figure 6.3) for a classroom experiment with three hypotheses and twelve weeks to conduct the experiment. If the classroom is the setting, clearly the students should be involved in establishing hypotheses, randomly selecting the variables for the week and studying the results with the teacher.

A.	+	+	+
B.	+	+	−
C.	+	−	+
D.	+	−	−
E.	−	+	+
F.	−	+	−
G.	−	−	+
H.	−	−	−

Figure 6.3 Design of experiments table.

Here is an example of a classroom DOE for spelling. This 12-week sequence for DOE can be carried out three different times during the school year.

Step 1. Determine three instructional variables to be studied. For example, worksheets, spelling buddies to teach each other, and classification activities (classify words with Venn diagrams, matrices, or in columns).

Step 2. Randomly select order of eight weeks. For example, write numbers one to eight on eight different sheets of paper. Place them in a bowl. Each Friday afternoon one student selects the next number. The class views the chart and notes spelling activities for the following week. For example the week that +, −, + is chosen, the students will have worksheet and classification assignments. There will be no buddy teaching.

Step 3. Carry out the experiment. For example, the teacher and students proceed through the weeks completing the assignments selected from the random pick of one to eight.

Step 4. Study results. For example, after each week's spelling test, study the success of students. Hopefully strategies described in *Improving Student Learning* are in place and the Friday spelling test is actual knowledge of spelling, not Thursday night crammed words.

Step 5. Reflect upon results. For example, take the week with the best spelling results and follow this exact same plan for the next four weeks to see if it makes sense and is the best sequence of activities for this particular class of students.

CONCLUSION

People do learn from experience; however, being mentored and systematically testing out new concepts are better teachers. I propose the sequence from most effective to least effective is (1) testing theory, (2) being mentored, and (3) experience.

Key Recommendation

Create a team of people interested in the outcome of experiments rather than a divided set of people disagreeing over today's new "flavor."

NO

Experience alone

Common sense alone

YES

Testing theory

Being mentored

7
No Clear Aim

Idon't think I've ever worked in an urban environment where "no clear aim" was not the number one frustration. These educators are given a new superintendent every few years and a new federal grant to implement several times a year. It is not uncommon for a school to have three or four different principals in a five-year period.

Readers who are from the rural or suburban communities cannot relax, however. *No clear aim* is perceived to be one of the top three problems outside urban centers. Whenever *permission to forget* or *always the ref, rarely the coach* are listed near the top, I realize here's a stable environment struggling with system issues.

ROOT CAUSE #7
Having no clear aim

Education has vision statements, mission statements, goals, and five-year plans. How could it be that people working within the system view having no clear aim as such a problem? I think it is because none of these statements give a clear aim. Once in a while one hears *aim* in the plural, but that is unusual. So part of the power of the word *aim* is that it is normally a singular word. Organizations can have many goals, but one aim. Ford Motor Company's aim, worked out with Deming in 1980, is as good an example as any. The aim of Ford is to produce cars that please the customer.

I am not opposed to vision statements and mission statements. I would prefer to place all of them on a target with the aim being the bull's-eye, and the other statements and goals finding their place on various rings of the target. The aim needs to be as simple as the Ford example. The best education aim, in my opinion, is simply to increase success; decrease failure. Elmore writes, "Organizations that improve do so because they create and nurture agreement on what is worth achieving, and they set in motion the internal processes by which people progressively know to do what they need to do in order to achieve what is worthwhile."[1] An aim is agreement upon what is worthwhile. "Senior leaders are the only people in the organization with a whole system perspective, positional power, and the resource control needed to determine both strategy and action."[2]

EDUCATION IS NOT ALONE

It is not only education and business that need a clear aim; government needs one also. In his book *Leadership,* Giuliani writes, "For years, the statistics in the Police Department that drew the most attention were the number of arrests and the reaction times to emergency calls. In fact, neither is the ultimate goal of a police force: public safety and reducing crime." He also wrote, "I insisted that everyone on my staff should concentrate on the core purpose of whichever agency or division we oversaw." Once the core purpose of an organization was identified, the next job was to align resources and focus on that purpose.[3] Deming, in his usual succinct manner wrote, "A system requires an aim. Without an aim, there is no system."[4] If there is no system what is there? One has a collection of parts, but not a system that works. And the collection of parts is called *status quo.*

SCHOOL DISTRICT AIM

The aim of a school district is to increase student success and decrease student failure. It is crucial that districts adopt an aim and bring all resources toward achievement of the aim. Districts need to have centralized strategic decisions and decentralized tactical decisions.[5] Too often districts ignore their responsibility for strategic leadership and then attempt to mandate the tactical decisions. It doesn't work. The staff in the schools resent and subvert the tactical decisions. "The result of this unfocused leadership is that the resources available are scattered in so many directions that no initiatives get the time, attention, and resources that are necessary for success."[6] Agreement with staff on the aim is a key centralized, strategic leadership responsibility.

It is quite interesting that research has shown the dynamics of motivation as being "two competing forces or drives—the striving for success and the fear of failure. Both drives operate simultaneously."[7]

After schools determine what is failure and what is success, then everybody is to work as a team to reduce failure and increase success. Deming labeled this *optimization.* He wrote, "Optimization is a process of orchestrating the efforts of all components toward achievement of the stated aim. Optimization means accomplishment of the aim: everybody gains. . . . Management's responsibility is to strive toward optimization of the system through time."[8] For example, if a state has a direct writing exam in a particular grade, the papers are often evaluated on a 1–4 scale with an average score being posted. A better approach would be to agree that a 1 paper is failure and a 3 or 4 is success. Then year after year, the staff is striving to have more successful students and fewer students experiencing failure. In Indiana, results are returned to school districts informing them how many students did not pass, how many achieved pass, and how many are at the level pass+. This designation is far superior to mere averages. Figure 7.1 displays the results of Riddle Elementary School in Rochester, Indiana. The descending line shows the percent of students designated, on the state exam, as did not pass. After Indiana added the pass+ on the state reports, the school was able to add the success line.

The opposite of optimization is suboptimization, which means a portion of the organization wins at the expense of the whole organization. Without a clear aim and alignment of people, equipment, materials, and other resources, departmental factions take over, meaning some win and some

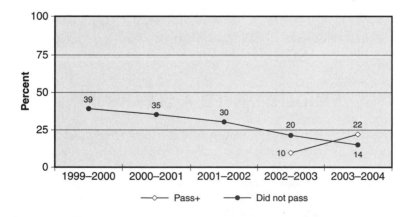

Figure 7.1 Graph showing the percentage of sixth-grade students who did not pass the state math exam and those who were at the pass+ level.

lose. At a 2004 Arizona Diamondbacks baseball game, a foul ball was hit into the stands. One fan raised up his 32-ounce beer and caught the foul ball in the beer. About 20 surrounding fans immediately began mopping the beer off their faces and clothes. (All were facing the foul ball.) One fan won a ball; all other fans lost. This baseball example illustrates what happens without a clear aim and everybody working together to accomplish that aim.

Without a clear aim, schools are whipsawed by changing direction. That is the reason the press reports stories like the following about science. "California's fourth- and eighth-graders scored worst in the country on a national science test released last month, and no one involved in the education system—parents, teachers, students, administrators—seemed particularly surprised. In recent years, reading, writing, and math have become a major priority for public schools and science lessons have dwindled. In some schools, it simply isn't taught. But there is no consequence for leaving it out."[9] A clear aim can keep school systems focused regardless of the outside pressure.

One reason that merit pay makes no sense for education is it takes away the team aspect of increasing success and decreasing failure. Some teachers who are clearly better at decreasing failure and now volunteer for more than their share of struggling students would no longer make that decision under merit pay. When a school district has the agreed upon aim of increasing success and decreasing failure and has spent the time to define each, opportunities for teamwork abound. Faculties can agree on definitions of success and failure for attendance, discipline, every school subject (both information and performance), extracurricular activities, student leadership, or whatever else is important. The goal is to have more students meeting the criteria for success and fewer meeting the criteria for failure. It matters not which team members contribute the most; it only matters that the school is making continuous improvement.

STUDENTS NEED A CLEAR AIM

I learned from Jeff Burgard, author of *Continuous Improvement in the Science Classroom*, former teacher, and now educational consultant, a most wonderful seminar activity. I use it as often as possible. Participants are placed in groups of four to seven with a 24-piece children's puzzle. They are first timed on putting together the puzzle face down and then piecing it together right-side-up with the advantage of following the picture on the box cover. Adults can always put the puzzle together faster when they see where they are going (the picture.)

For students it is the same. Their clear aim is a list of key concepts to be learned for the course and the rubrics by which their performance assignments will be measured. Students view a class as "hard" when they spend more time attempting to figure out what they are supposed to learn rather than actually learning. An "easy" course is one where learning expectations are clear from day one. Students need help making a distinction between the "two types of knowledge—declarative and procedural, where declarative knowledge is more information based, procedural knowledge is more skill or process based."[10] Further, these students need to view examples of the expectations. These examples are from prior students, with the names removed. If the work is written, it can be scanned and posted on the teacher's Web site. If it is three-dimensional, then with digital cameras, educators can take several pictures of prior projects and post them on the Internet. The point is to make as clear as possible the expectations for the end of the course. Show students sample 1 papers and projects, sample 2 work, 3s, and 4s. Highly visible standards, not highly secret standards, are needed. Research has shown that "Learning is enhanced when a teacher identifies specific types of knowledge that are the focus of a unit or lesson."[11] As Douglas Reeves reminds us, clear expectation "affords not only educational excellence, but also equity of opportunity."[12]

In addition to an overall aim, students deserve to have a clear aim for each subject. Michael Thompson provides a clear example. The aim of literature study that he suggests is, "to know the mind of the world, and to join the long argument into which they (the students) were born." To accomplish this, he writes, students must "read the classics . . . knowing current books—even the best—is not the same as knowing the history of ideas."[13]

I also suggest that students who attended a course last year are a great source for communicating the aim with pinpoint accuracy. For example, first-grade teachers can invite two of their students from the prior year to read to this year's first-graders. The students should be ones who started first grade reading only a few words and commercial signs and ended the year reading around 60 words per minute on end-of-first-grade material. By having a boy and a girl read to the new first-graders, these six-year-olds can hold in their minds' eye the big picture for first-grade reading.

AIM FOR FINANCE, PERSONNEL, AND OPERATIONS

In addition to learning, this same aim works for all aspects of a school district: operations, finance, and personnel. Each function of educating and managing a school district should have this same aim. Operations such as transportation and maintenance can readily determine success and failure for each of their responsibilities. For example, in maintenance, failure can be a work order that has over a week response time and success can be a one-day completion of work. Over time, the organization can work to achieve more successes and fewer failures. One aspect of personnel is to have more teachers who meet the needs of all or almost all of their students and fewer who meet the needs of nobody. This can be accomplished through vastly improved recruitment practices, such as those provided by Ventures for Excellence, and by having a better documentation of poor performance, when necessary.[14] (Noguera reported, "We also asked students if they believed their teachers were really concerned about how well they did in school. Disturbingly, 56 percent of the students said they did not believe their teachers really cared.")[15]

Finance is another area that fits very nicely into the aim of increasing success and decreasing failure. Success in finance is spending money on activities and objects that positively impact student learning. Failure is spending money on items that do not have an impact upon learning, or, if these expenses were reduced, learning would not be damaged. First, the list of failure items has to be agreed upon. Next, the cost per pupil has to be calculated. For example, as a superintendent I was appalled to learn that we spent over $10 per year per child on garbage pickup. I had seen the total figure before, but until it was listed as a per child number, it didn't really sink into my brain. So, success is increasing the money spent on expenditures that impact learning, such as library books or music instruments. Decreasing failure is reducing the cost of each expenditure that adds no value to learning. The failure items will not go away, but they can be reduced. Schools will need insurance and attorneys, for example. With concerted efforts, however, costs per pupil can be reduced. If a school district is growing in enrollment, merely holding costs as a constant can reduce the cost per pupil.

Another reason for calculating cost per pupil is so superintendents and business officials can learn more easily from each other. Large, medium, and small districts can talk together, compare their garbage pickup costs, and learn from each other. Business literature on lean organizations can be of great help to educators in reducing these costs. Too often we have lean classrooms and do not have a lean trash pickup budget item. In an interview conducted by Greg Hutchins, Norman Bodek, sometimes called the father of lean, states, "A rising economic tide floats all boats, including the marginally efficient, hiding inefficiencies and waste. But a lean company is best positioned to be successful during an economic slowdown. In these times, successful companies are those that can operate with the highest quality at the lowest cost, eliminating all waste."[16]

SCHOOL BOARDS

One of the most difficult aspects of creating and maintaining a clear aim is the politics of the local board of education. It is the responsibility of the board to come to agreement on the aim and to do everything within its power to help the superintendent achieve the aim. One of the joys of my superintendent experience was having Gloria Valles as my board president for 10 years. She knew her job was to help me, and thus all employees and students, increase success and decrease failure. Education does not need board members determined to have their own way who suboptimize the whole district. One school board member can hold up the "32 ounces of beer" and soak hundreds of people.

PRODUCTIVITY

Business leaders often find that productivity of schools is hard to measure. Why is this so? It is because there is no clear aim. If every year there is a new program, a ton of new laws, a new direction, and a new accountability plan, there is no way to measure productivity. In addition, exams change at the whim of state boards of education every five years or so, so data over time are very difficult to obtain. Having a clear aim and bringing all resources to bear on the aim will allow productivity to be measured.

PLANNING DOCUMENTS

I recommend the fishbone diagram as the tool for the cover of educational planning documents. The fishbone diagram is fairly well known in education, but is rarely printed as the first page of a school or school district improvement plan. It is more often considered a clever tool for teachers to use with students (which it is). The fishbone diagram shown in Figure 7.2 has four pairs of main bones. The four main bones are for each of the four major functions of the school district: learning, personnel, finance, and operations. The aim is inscribed inside the head of the fish: increase success; decrease failure.

The blanks on the subbones are for adding enough district activities so that all employees know their responsibilities are noted on the fishbone. Page numbers are then placed after each subbone so users of the planning document can easily find the details of the school district planning document.

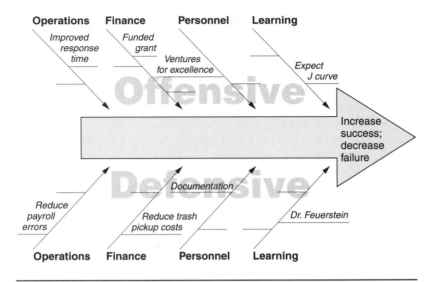

Figure 7.2 Fishbone diagram cover for school district planning document.

My only addition to known fishbone diagram knowledge is to add the labels *offensive* and *defensive* to the upper and lower regions of the fishbone. Offensive is increasing success and defensive is decreasing failure. These responsibilities must be separated as the people carrying out the various functions have different skill sets. For example, the person working with a community to pass a bond for technology is usually different from the person working to lower the costs of trash pickup.

MONITORING THE PLAN

Once the board has approved the planning document, the responsibility of administration is to carry out the plans. One way to assist in the management of the many different activities is to label each activity with a one to six reporting level. The six levels are:

1. Report in person weekly.

2. Report by e-mail weekly.

3. Report in person monthly.

4. Report by e-mail monthly.

5. Report in person quarterly.

6. Report by e-mail quarterly.

Such a system, or variation, will certainly assist the board in knowing there is a plan to carry out the document and there will be fewer surprises when the annual review occurs. Likewise it will assist employees in knowing their exact reporting responsibility.

MEASURING SUCCESS AND FAILURE

The radar chart is the perfect graph for end-of-the-year reporting. A vector for each subbone can be created. The data for each subbone must all be converted to percentages from zero percent to 100 percent for the radar chart to display results for all initiatives on one graph. Figures 7.3 and 7.4 show two years of data on radar charts. When creating a radar chart, each

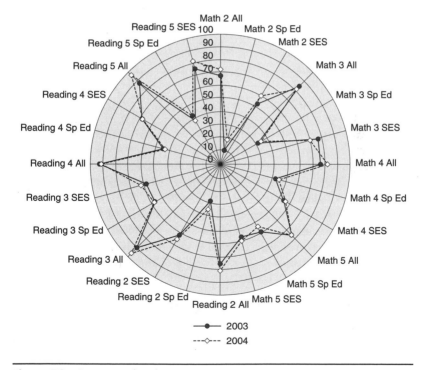

Figure 7.3 Success radar chart.

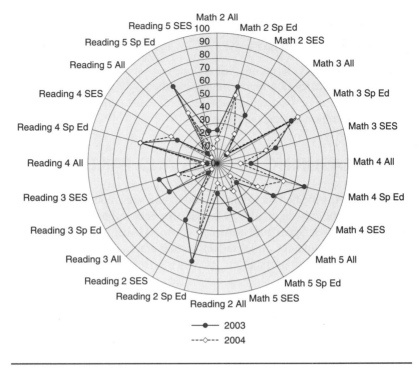

Figure 7.4 Failure radar chart.

line on an Excel spreadsheet becomes a vector on the radar chart. One radar chart displays success, with the goal being 100 percent success—all dots at the outer edge of the radar chart. The other radar chart measures reduction of failure with the goal being to have a clump of dots at the very center. One does not want a failure dot to be readily visible.

On the radar chart, one can clearly discern backwards motion because the lines will cross, showing fewer successes or more failures than in prior years. If the radar chart is printed on 11 × 17 tabloid paper, school districts can display and understand five years of data on the two charts.

CONCLUSION

Without a clear aim that is understood by all, organizations waste everyone's time. It is easy to see what occurs when five school board members, a superintendent, and a union create seven different versions of the ideal future. Chaos occurs. This lack of focus can occur at every level—federal, state, district, school, and classroom. The aim to increase success and decrease failure can have significant impact at all levels of education.

Key Recommendations

Start with a clear aim; it is the bull's-eye. Keep it simple and prominent. The job of the manager is to help everybody know how they contribute to the aim. Clearly state what success is and what failure is for every aspect of school district responsibility.

NO

Random acts

Next good idea

YES

Increasing success; decreasing failure

Clear, common aim

8

Poor Psychology

It is not the responsibility of teachers to motivate students. In spite of the fact that Education 101 and Psychology 101 admonish educators to motivate students, it still is not the responsibility of teachers to motivate students. When teachers first hear this statement, they have one of two reactions. The first is, "Yes, that's right. It's the parent's responsibility to motivate and my job to teach." The second reaction is, "This cannot be accurate. Students don't learn if they are not motivated and it's therefore my job to motivate them."

Both reactions are wrong. Students enter education already motivated. Look at any kindergarten classroom; it is full of motivated students. It is the responsibility of educators to determine what is causing students to lose their motivation and stop such practices. Students do not need the teachers' money to buy stickers, pizza, and other incentives. What they need are the teachers' ears. What is causing children to lose their motivation for learning?

ROOT CAUSE #8
Poor psychology

THE ENTHUSIASM TIMETABLE

I reported in *Improving Student Learning* my discovery regarding the timetable of this loss of enthusiasm. I had assumed, incorrectly, that elementary schools managed to keep enthusiasm high and it was lost in middle and high schools. Wrong. Dead wrong. Enthusiasm is lost at each and every grade in equal increments. Society doesn't notice this loss until middle school when half of the students would prefer to not be in school, but the loss does not begin in middle school.

Suppose a kindergarten teacher receives 24 students, all of whom are excited to enter kindergarten. It is very likely that 23 of the 24 will be very excited to enter first-grade one year later. The teacher only lost the enthusiasm of one student. The first-grade teacher receives 24 students, 23 of whom are thrilled to be in first grade. This teacher, nine months later, sends on to second grade 21 students who are thrilled with school. Now there are three students who would rather not be in school. Statistically, this doesn't seem so bad unless you are the parent or grandparent of one of the three. When this slight loss is repeated over 13 years, it is easy to see that few students are thrilled with school when they are in high school.

Stopping this loss of enthusiasm for learning is a huge challenge. It is not the responsibility of educators to motivate students to learn. They come to school already motivated. It is, however, the responsibility of all who work in the school environment (teachers, administrators, secretaries, cooks, custodians, bus drivers) to help determine what is causing this loss and then band together to stop these practices.

The loss of enthusiasm progression is described by both Senge and Phillip Schlechty: Senge's continuum is (1) genuine compliance, (2) formal compliance, (3) grudging compliance, (4) noncompliance, and, finally, (5) apathy.[1] Schlechty has identified the stages of loss of enthusiasm as (1) authentic engagement, (2) ritual engagement, (3) passive compliance, (4) retreatism, and (5) rebellion.[2]

EDUCATION IS DETERMINED TO BRIBE BOTH ADULTS AND CHILDREN

"In Fairfax's Excel schools, when the school achieves its target, everyone in the school gets a bonus (up to $2000 just before the holidays in December)."[3]

"Kansas City school board members vigorously debated the idea of rewarding students for test scores Wednesday before voting 6–3 to approve an almost $380,000 incentive package. The majority of board members think giving schools incentives of up to $80 a student will boost state test scores."[4]

"Chicago public schools that show the most improvement on their standardized test scores will receive $10,000 as part of a new system of incentives that focuses on raising test scores."[5]

"Tickets to sporting events and coupons for Walgreen's drug stores are among the incentives that will be offered to Chicago public high school students this year to get them to show up for class more often. Some kids likened the idea to bribes, but Chicago Schools CEO Arne Duncan said he was merely trying to 'incent improvement.' "[6]

Even the federal government is involved in incentivizing our youth. "The Department of Education announced 11 sites across the country that will participate in the No Child Left Behind Act's Summer Reading Achievement Program. To take part, students in grades K–8 must read 10 or more books over the summer and fill out paperwork about what they learned from each book. Successful students will earn prizes and certificates."[7]

Schools that are determined to give rewards to students and public officials determined to give rewards to teachers should know they are acting with great arrogance. They are essentially saying, "I am self-motivated, but you yokels at the bottom of the food chain are lazy and need a kick in the pants. I will motivate you." The reaction to this arrogance can be predicted. Senge writes, "People with a sense of their own vision and commitment would naturally reject efforts of a leader to 'get them committed.' "[8]

I have to wonder how motivated teachers are when they open up the paper and read, "The state Department of Education may have to reclaim $750,000 it mistakenly awarded to some Fresno county schools after a scoring error on a standardized test." In an understatement, the president of a local union said, "We have some mad people."[9]

For people reading this book that are considering incentives as just described, please be prepared for disappointment. "No reward system has even been invented that people in an organization haven't learned how to 'game.' "[10]

I am well aware that much of the pressure to give incentives to public employees and their students comes from people employed in business. The incentive system does not work in business either. "We found no systematic pattern linking specific forms of executive compensation to the process of going from good to great. The idea that the structure of executive compensation is a key driver in corporate performance is simply not supported by the data."[11]

THE WHOLE SYSTEM

One of the difficulties of education is seeing the whole system at once. One can tour a factory in a portion of a day and see the raw materials enter and the manufactured product emerge. Depending on whether or not one counts college, education is a 13- to 17-year experience, making observation of the whole system quite complex. For example, kindergarten and first-grade teachers making a retention decision do not have a high school teacher on the committee. Why would this be important? Every retention in kindergarten and first grade creates a 19-year-old high school senior. The teacher of seniors can relate to the committee what it is like to be 19 in high school. This does not mean that retention is always the wrong decision. Without the knowledge of the complete system, however, teachers cannot be expected to make the best decisions.

Incentives are yet another example of another set of decisions made without full knowledge of the system. I have asked teachers in many states to verify my numbers, and they state I'm generally correct. It is quite normal in elementary grades for teachers to offer incentives five times a day. This includes stickers, reminders about the upcoming pizza party for meeting a goal, marbles in a jar for accomplishments, and so forth. In middle and high schools about five times a day a student asks, "Does this count?" In other words, if I do this work will it count on my grade?

If students are offered incentives five times a day for 180 days for 13 years (kindergarten through grade 12), this adds up to 11,700 incentives. If the theory behind incentives is accurate, then our high school seniors would be the most motivated people on the face of the earth. Clearly, they are not. The incentive process started in kindergarten does not work for 13 years; it is a failure.

DO GRADES MOTIVATE?

Deci writes, "In education, grades are the primary means of extrinsic control. They are considered incentives, and it is assumed that people will be motivated to learn so they can get good grades. In one learning experiment I did with former student Carl Benware, we considered the issue of grades as a motivator. We had two groups of college students spend about three hours learning some complex material on neurophysiology—on the machinery of the brain. Half of these students were told they would be tested and graded on their learning, and the others were told they would have the opportunity to put the material to active use by teaching it to others. We expected that learning in order to be tested would feel very controlling to the students, whereas learning to put the information to active use would feel like an exciting challenge. After students had learned the material, we assessed their intrinsic motivation with a questionnaire, and we found, as expected, that those who learned in order to be tested were less intrinsically motivated.

"Then we took it one step further to get at the main issue—the actual learning that had gone on. We tested both groups, even though one group had not expected it, and the results showed that the students who learned in order to put the material to active use displayed considerably greater conceptual understanding of the material than did the students who learned in order to be tested. As the research made clear, yet again, well-intentioned people—for instance, people employing tests to motivate learning—are unwittingly defeating the desire to learn in those people they are attempting to help."[12]

What Deci reported for college students is reported by Collins for adults. It seems this is true for people of all ages. "Expending energy trying to motivate people is largely a waste of time. The real question then becomes: How do you manage in such a way as not to demotivate people?"[13]

THE FIVE-YEAR-OLD ENTERING KINDERGARTEN

On a consulting trip to Chile I heard about a five-year-old student who spoke four languages. His father always spoke to him in Arabic, his mother in French, his neighbors in Spanish, and his teachers in English. This is a normal brain with an incredible opportunity. Schools need to think of their entering kindergartners as people with incredible brains, much information and knowledge to gain, in need of help with character development and wisdom and as having all of the motivation they will need for life. Educators are to assist parents with character development and wisdom, they are to provide significant information and knowledge, but they are not to motivate. The motivation is an incredible asset, already present, that is to be protected.

When one of my granddaughters came home from her first day of kindergarten with a sticker on her dress, this wonderful, well-meaning teacher was unintentionally reaching into a five-year-old's heart to remove the intrinsic motivation and replace it with extrinsic motivation. The teacher did not see that her job was to protect the motivation already present. She was motivating her students, as instructed in college courses.

FOUR CONCEPTUAL UNDERSTANDINGS

Four conceptual understandings are necessary to protect motivation of students. They are basic Piaget, the difference between celebration and reward, invidious compliments, and the climate for maintaining enthusiasm.

Basic Piaget

Jean Piaget, the Swiss epistemologist, taught us that children do not think as adults, but they feel exactly like adults. David Elkind expresses this the best: "One of the most serious and pernicious misunderstandings about young children is that they are most like adults in their thinking and least like us in their feelings. In fact, just the reverse is true, and children are most like us in their feelings and least like us in their thinking."[14]

It takes no psychology courses to understand how children feel. They feel exactly like adults feel. For example, let's assume that it's May and two teachers are planning for next year. One says that students will learn more math if they are grouped by ability. The suggestion is made that one teacher instruct the best math students, the second one instruct the middle group, and the new teacher (yet to be hired) teach the lower group. The second teacher replies, "Won't students feel badly having to pick up their books and move to a different room for math?" The first teacher replies, "Oh no, they won't mind, they are just kids."

This thinking is dead wrong. They will mind. There is no such thing as a pattern for feeling development. One cannot say students feel this way from birth to two, feel another way from two to seven, then feel like this from seven to 12, and finally begin to feel like adults after 12 or so. Students feel like their teachers feel.

In a Missouri classroom in 2003, a teacher became very frustrated with a student ignoring her admonitions to clean out his desk. So one morning when the second-grader arrived in school he found his desk on its side with the contents strewn across the room. How did the student feel? He felt exactly the same as a teacher walking into the staff room and finding the contents of his mailbox strewn across the staff room with a note taped on the mailbox. The note says, "In spite of repeated requests to clean out your mailbox, you have not done so. We cannot put any new announcements in your box. (Copy in personnel file.)"

Students know the difference between being chastised in front of their peers and having a teacher who says, "Step out in the hallway, I need to speak with you." Teachers know the difference between a private discussion in the principal's office and an embarrassing comment made in the staff meeting. (As Michael Thompson wrote, educators must at the very minimum promise students, "I will make sure that no one is embarrassed.")[15]

It is fairly obvious that if the bus drivers, cooks, custodians, secretaries, librarians, nurses, coaches, counselors, administrators, and teachers treat students as if their feelings are different from their own, and if this treatment lasts for 13 years, students won't like school very much.

As I have said repeatedly in this book, I am not in any way writing to criticize educators. What I am attempting to debunk is the advice that educators have received to motivate their students. The advice is terrible. When educators internalize that students do not think like they think, but feel like they feel, a major step forward will have been taken. Much less enthusiasm will be lost.

Reward versus Celebration

An excellent, though not perfect, synonym for reward is *bribe* whereas the best synonym for celebration is *thank you.* The reward systems in place in our classrooms are causing students to lose interest in school. Deci is America's expert on how the extrinsic motivators actually cause people to lose intrinsic motivation. His book, *Why We Do What We Do* is a must-read for anyone halfway interested in fascinating research documenting how extrinsic motivation destroys intrinsic motivation.

Nevertheless, there is everything to be gained and nothing to be lost by having adults thank students for their hard work and successes. People know the difference between a thank you and a contrived reward system designed to control them. After a particularly successful exam, an Indiana teacher asked one student to place a message in the principal's voice mail detailing their success. When the student was through recording, the class applauded and then all returned to work. This is but one of many clever ways I've heard of teachers expressing thanks. It is not a bribe—"If you do well on the quiz, I'll let one of you call the principal." Calling the principal is not going to motivate middle school students. However, a spontaneous thank you is accepted and appreciated.

The difference between reward and celebration is one of inner motive. The reward system says, "I don't trust these kids, they need to be controlled and incentives control." The celebration system says, "I have the greatest class of students. I can trust them completely to do quality work and cooperate with me and others. I don't want to take them for granted, so I will show my appreciation of them by saying 'thank you.' " Kids know instantly the difference between a loving thank you and a controlling reward system.

Invidious Compliments

"Once you understand what an invidious compliment is (a compliment that includes one person and excludes another, leaving the outsider looking [vid] in [in] enviously), you become acutely conscious of the hurt that invidious praise causes—and be careful not to do it," writes Michael Thompson.[16]

Many times the reason students lose their enthusiasm for learning is they are subjected to numerous invidious compliments such as, "I like the way Jasmine is sitting."

Climate for Maintaining Enthusiasm

The climate for maintaining enthusiasm is described by Carson and Burgard in their books.[17] I am not duplicating their work here, but will state the essence. They have a structured listening approach for collecting data monthly on student enthusiasm, listing suggestions for improvement, conducting class meetings on improvement suggestions, and making changes each month based on what students say. They have documented that students really do want the ears of their teachers much more than their money for pizza and popcorn. If all they are offered is food, they will take it, but having their suggestions for classroom improvement implemented is much more lasting than a few calories. The calories will be forgotten, but the students will remember as adults the day they suggested in seventh grade that they would learn more if the teacher reworded certain key concepts and the teacher took the suggestion.

The essence of what Carson and Burgard can teach is captured by the following statement to the students: "This year I will not be motivating you. What I will be doing is listening to any school event prior to this year that caused you to lose your motivation, and I will be listening to anything I might do that causes you to lose motivation. My aim is to restore the level of motivation you had in kindergarten." Noguera writes almost the exact same thoughts. "If we were more willing to listen and solicit their opinions, we might find ways to engage students more deeply in their own education."[18]

Duane Schiestel, as a student in Turnberry Central Public School (Ontario, Canada), in 1996 conducted fairly sophisticated research comparing student and faculty perceptions of the top causes for improvement in education. Both faculty and students selected the top nine from a list of 30 controllable factors. The two Pareto charts (Figures 8.1 and 8.2) show the differences between the faculty and student perceptions. For example, class size was a much bigger issue for faculty than students. This book does not purport to state which is correct, but to provide the reader a chance to (1) see the value of student input and (2) study the differences in perception between adults and students.

The 2003 Malcolm Baldrige National Quality Award winners, Community Consolidated School District 15, Palatine, Illinois schools, implemented the concepts taught by Carson and Burgard and had a 50 percent increase in third-grade reading enthusiasm and a 100 percent increase in fifth-grade

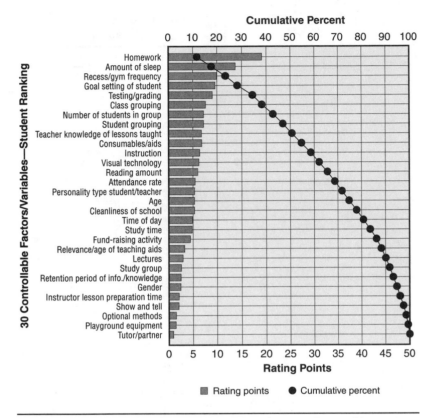

Figure 8.1 Thirty controllable factors—Pareto chart, student ranking.

and eighth-grade reading enthusiasm.[19] Figures 8.3 to 8.5 provide the exact results. The data were compiled by asking students to check a happy face, straight face, or sad face for each school subject. Figure 8.3 shows the percentage of happy faces for six years. The decline is from over 80 percent in kindergarten in 1997–2001 to approximately 25 percent in eighth grade. Five years later the loss is almost stopped. Figure 8.4 starts with the 1997–98 school year, which is when Palatine began the enthusiasm data collection. Each line is a grade level, graphed year to year. It is not until the 2001–02 school year when Carson and Burgard's methodology was attempted. Figure 8.5 aggregates the data from each separate grade level in Figure 8.4 into one enthusiasm line averaging all grade levels.

"The starvation of the imagination is one of the most fruitful sources of exhaustion and sapping in a worker's life."[20] This quote from the 1910s

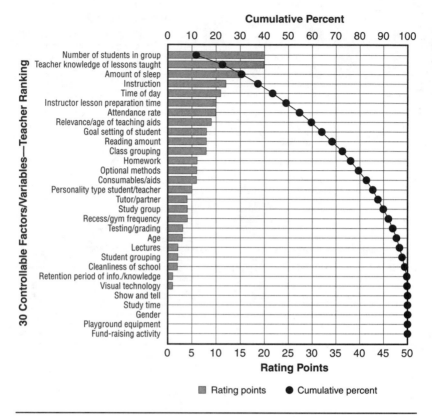

Figure 8.2   Thirty controllable factors—Pareto chart, teacher ranking.

describes well what the continual series of bribes does to the joy of learning in school.

"What do the right people want more than anything else? They want to be a part of a winning team. They want to contribute to producing visible, tangible results. They want to feel the excitement of being involved in something that just flat-out works."[21] Collins wrote this for adults; it is equally true for children. *Improving Student Learning* concepts provide exactly what Collins is talking about for children. A scoreboard for the class, acting as a team, is posted and celebrated. Children want to be a part of a classroom team that flat-out works!

Another piece of wise advice, in regard to restoring motivation, is to "create great memories" and "make someone's day."[22] Remember it is not praise that is going to create this needed climate for learning. Students see through continual praise as an attempt to control. "The praise is intended as

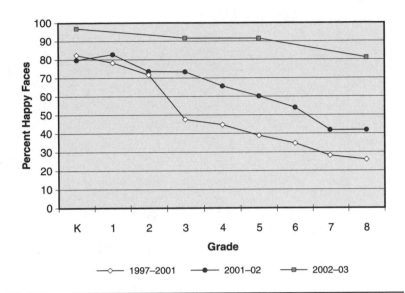

Figure 8.3 Palatine increase in enthusiasm.

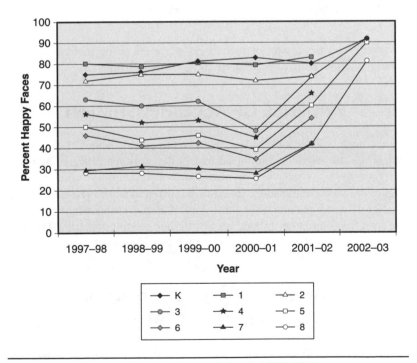

Figure 8.4 Palatine enthusiasm by grade level, 1997–2003.

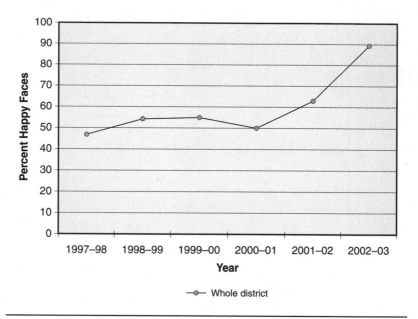

Figure 8.5   Palatine enthusiasm, all together.

a reward, and the giving of rewards is supposed to be motivating—two ideas that could hardly be more obviously wrong, yet persist."[23]

EVIDENCE OF ACCOMPLISHMENT

"To be intrinsically motivated, people need to perceive themselves as competent and autonomous; they need to feel that they are effective and self-determining. Someone else's opinion does not do the trick."[24] For example, Figure 8.6 shows the reading speed of a third-grader who started the year, reading 10 words per minute on third-grade material. He ended the year reading over 100 words per minute on third-grade reading material. This evidence of success is far more powerful than any amount of stickers, money, popcorn, or attaboys.

IMPORTANCE OF ADDRESSING ENTHUSIASM

Marzano states it best, "The link between student motivation and achievement is straightforward. If students are motivated to learn the content in a

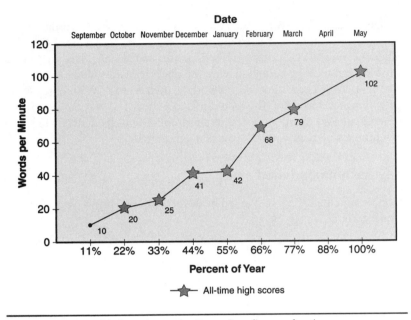

Figure 8.6   One third-grade student's reading fluency for the year.

given subject, their achievement in that subject most likely will be good. If students are not motivated to learn the content, their achievement will likely be limited."[25] Thirty to 60 minutes per month to address motivation, as described by Carson and Burgard, will reap great benefits. The time taken away from instruction to deal with motivation will be repaid over and over by students more excited about learning.

CONCLUSION

Carolyn Ayres, author of *Continuous Improvement in the Mathematics Classroom*, wrote me, "I have a class graph on the wall of the total number of high frequency words students in the class can read. (First grade). After the November check, I talked to my new eighth-grade student helper and asked her to take on with me having students make big gains in reading the words. I set up some games she could play with a small group, and grouped the students according to which set of 25 words they should be working on. My aide was the only one that worked with the students in this area up until I did the December check. The graph jumped up dramatically. I showed the student the graph and told her that she was the main change in instruction and we could conclude that she should be credited with the big jump in students reading the words. She was so jazzed! It was the last day before Christmas vacation, and not only that, the last ten minutes of that day. Students were busy finishing up their party, and no one was thinking of anything but packing up and leaving the place for two weeks. The student aide said, 'May I take some kids to work on their words?' Would I say 'No?' Of course not. I asked, 'Who would like to go work with Amanda?' Hands went up all over the room. She took three children to the hallway to grab a few minutes on their words." Now that's motivation!

Key Recommendation

Stop motivating. Protect the enthusiasm students bring with them to kindergarten.

NO
Incentives
Bribes

YES
Listening
Celebrations

9

Always the Referee, Rarely the Coach

"Why do you want to become a teacher," was the familiar question in the interview. The answer surprised the interview panel as the applicant replied, "I can hardly wait until Saturdays to grade papers."

I have never heard this answer in an interview. In fact almost every answer to this question can be classified as a "coach" answer, not a "referee" answer. Teachers select their profession based on a desire to help students learn. They do not envision themselves in 10 years sitting on the team bus grading papers with a flashlight, however, the referee responsibility is overcoming the innate coaching desire in many of our teachers.

The referee responsibility is appropriate. Students and parents do have a right to know how well they are performing. There are two significant flaws, however, with the current reporting system. They are (1) a belief in 100 percent inspection and (2) a lack of understanding of the power of feedback to students. "The role of the school is not to announce a judgment but to coach improvement."[1]

ROOT CAUSE #9

*Always the referee,
rarely the coach*

A high school teacher's math classroom has four walls of whiteboard with barely enough space for two bulletin boards. When I inquired as to why this learning environment, the teacher replied that her classroom structure was quite traditional. The typical day was (1) review of yesterday's work, (2) introduction to today's new content, (3) sample problems completed by her, (4) guided practice by a few students, and then (5) time for students to practice. Her major difference in organization was that students worked in pairs at the whiteboard instead of alone at their desks. The reasons for this change were, she can stand anywhere in the room to see exactly how the practice is transpiring and she can stand next to students and listen to their math conversation. She said that if she cannot hear them think she is handicapped in helping them solve the math.

I was so impressed with this structure, but was soon brought to an emotional low. The teacher explained how she loved her job, loved teaching all day, and couldn't imagine a better job, however, she was about to stop this practice. Her reward for teaching all day, every day was a huge stack of homework to grade every night. She couldn't keep up. I asked her what other math teachers do about the homework problem and was informed that they sit at their desk and grade papers while the students are practicing at their desks. I doubt that when these math teachers were being interviewed and were asked the standard question as to why they wanted to be a teacher that they answered, "I can hardly wait to sit at a desk all day and grade homework."

The referee responsibility is killing the enthusiasm of our teachers. They entered education to help students, not to be paper pushers. What is at the root of this problem? It is the false belief that quality can be inspected into a process. It cannot. Quality has to be built into the process. Teachers can spend years of their lives inspecting papers with no appreciable gain in quality of learning. It simply does not work. So what is the problem?

The problem is described in this hypothetical conversation with a teacher.

Lee: Are teachers generally pressured to use data to inform their instruction?

Teacher: Yes.

Lee: Are teachers using data to inform their teaching?

Teacher: Usually not.

Lee: Why not?

Teacher: No time.

Lee: Why no time?

Teacher: After I grade all those papers and prepare for the next day, the day is over.

The solution to the overburdening is item analysis and then teaching to the errors. First I am going to describe a method of building quality, assuming time is not an issue. Next, I'll give the realistic answer. The time-is-not-an-issue answer is to score all the homework papers and afterwards tally errors. Of the 120 papers scored, 83 made this error, 75 made this error, and so on. The teacher returns to the classroom the following day and states to the classroom, "I read all of your papers and they are being returned to you. I found that 83 made one error and 75 made a second error. So, I searched on the Internet last evening for a couple of hours and found two unique methods for teaching these concepts. Today we will be using these methods to learn what you missed." This is the solution for the teacher with no outside interests, no family, no athletic or activity responsibilities, and no graduate coursework.

The realistic answer involves sampling the papers; 100 percent inspection has to be eliminated. First I will share the process and then the theory why sampling is the solution. The sampling teacher selects five papers from each period of math and scores these five. The five are chosen randomly using tokens or some other random number generator. Teachers can use www.random.org, spreadsheets, dice, names in a hat, or graphing calculators. Each student has an equal chance of his or her paper being selected each and every assignment. The teacher explains, "After reading the 25 papers (five from each period), I found that 16 made one error and 14 made another error. Therefore I'll be teaching today based upon those errors. I realize I have taught this lesson before, but for some unknown reason you didn't learn it, so I've decided to attempt the lesson from another angle. I am returning all of your papers whether they were corrected or only checked off as turned in. If I did not correct your paper, look closely to see if you made the same error as two-thirds of your classmates. Remember, I am your coach for now. I want everyone to be successful. The time will come, closer to report card time, when I must score everyone's work for grading purposes. I'll be the referee then, but for now I'm the coach."

Such item analysis is essential for both performance assignments, such as writing, and informational assignments, such as math concepts, computation, and vocabulary. Teachers are responsible for the item analysis for the classroom as a whole and students are responsible for item analysis of their own work. Appendix C is a list of key concepts students are to learn in middle school science. Students have two responsibilities in regard to their data folder. One is to graph the number correct on weekly quizzes, the second is to highlight items on the key concept list that they answered correctly. Thus students are keeping their own individual item analysis. Any item not highlighted either has not been quizzed or was missed.

This explanation with students is crucial. Senge states it so well when he writes, "Leaders in learning organizations have the ability to conceptualize their strategic insights so that they become public knowledge, open to challenge and further improvements."[2] When teachers explain their feedback system to students and parents, they are putting into practice what Senge has described. Students and parents have the opportunity to challenge and help improve the learning classroom.

The good news is that it takes less time to score 25 papers and do the tally marks for the item analysis than it takes to inspect over 100 papers. The bad news is that the teacher cannot state that a particular concept has been taught and therefore it is taken care of for the year. If the item analysis shows students do not understand a concept, it has to be retaught and retaught and retaught until it is learned. It takes time to figure out new ways of explaining a concept. Time thinking about how to reteach an unlearned concept is being a coach. Time scoring over 100 papers night after night is being a referee. Coaching generates energy; refereeing drains energy.

Reeves writes, "A successful coach does not offer universal praise or condemnation but instead specific feedback. He is unequivocally clear about the mission and objectives and is, above all, a great teacher who identifies each step that takes the team from vision through execution to success."[3] The teacher as coach is not continually evaluating students with a grade, but continually providing feedback to students so they can excel. The teacher does not have the luxury of an outside referee; she is both coach and referee. She can, however, clearly draw a distinction between the two roles and be the referee only when necessary.

Thompson does not write about sampling, but does state the power of item analysis. "When I finish grading a stack of papers, I then tabulate the errors for all papers to find out what the most common errors were in the class as a whole, so that I can give a review lecture on the worst problems. The kids find it interesting to learn that in a class of eighteen, there were, say, twenty-two misplaced modifiers; when we go back over that concept, they take notes with new intensity."[4]

The theory behind such a process involves the understanding of system theory. Much has been written on the topic, most notably by Deming in *The New Economics*. System theory states that the job of the leader is to work on the system and the job of the workers is to work in the system. The teacher is to work on the system and the student has to work in the system. The student has no power to change the system; the teacher has the power to change the classroom system. By randomly selecting each day a sample of papers and tallying errors, the teacher is gaining a picture of the learning system. Grades in a grade book do not provide such a picture of the system. When teachers want to follow their hearts and become much more like coaches, they must accept their responsibility for continually improving the learning system in their classroom.

Improving the system depends upon the knowledge that "the most sophisticated test in the world is of limited value if a teacher cannot use the information to improve classroom practice. Announcing that math scores are low is not nearly as helpful as a report that helps teachers understand that their students are strong in mathematical calculation but weak in measurement, particularly in metric measurement."[5]

The second theoretical understanding for implementing such a system is basic variation. Variation always exists, and the two types of variation are special and common. When teachers greet their new students for a school year, they know that the students will vary in their abilities. Teachers will never have a class of students reading at the same level. Variation is always present. The knowledge that variation always exists is what fuels the responsibility to have 100 percent inspection. The second aspect of variation, however, is what takes away the need for 100 percent inspection. The two types of variation are common and special. Almost all variation is common, seldom is it special. When teachers read five papers from each period, they have knowledge of their system because almost all students are within their system and any variation among them is really common variation. When teachers read 100 percent of the papers, they are assuming all students are statistically special. They are humanly special, but not statistically special. Most students will learn more as the teachers improve the system. The students are in the system and will improve as the classroom system improves.

When the teachers take cramming out of the system, the students have no choice but to respond to a noncramming system. Likewise, when teachers take 100 percent inspection out of the system and replace it with a coaching system with referee activities near grading time, they will respond. Dave Scragg, of Regional Educational Service Agency (RESA) V in Parkersburg, West Virginia, reminds us that football practice is not graded, but the game is graded. Band practice is not graded, but the parade is graded. There is a time for being the referee, but the majority of our energy and time is to be spent on coaching so that we can create as many winners as possible.

The difference between feedback and evaluation is significant in this discussion. Students need far more feedback (a coaching responsibility) and far less evaluation (a referee responsibility). For the purposes of this discussion, grades are considered evaluation and specific error analysis is feedback. Thomas Guskey writes, "Teachers do need to check regularly on how students are doing, what they've learned, and what problems or difficulties they've experienced. But grading and reporting are different from checking; they involve judging the adequacy of students' performance at a specific time. Typically, teachers use checking to diagnose and prescribe and grading to evaluate and describe."[6] Research, as reported by Marzano, documents that feedback does improve learning, but must occur multiple times throughout the year.[7] Researchers use the term *formative* assessment to refer to feedback provided for improvement purposes and *summative* as evaluation provided for end-of-course grading. For example, when students write stories, the teacher may have a grade, editing comments, or both on the paper. Normally, when a grade is placed on the paper, the evaluation takes precedence over any editing comments. Students routinely glance at the grade and toss the paper. Feedback, however, is a completely different process. The teacher says this paper was written for practice. He reads five papers from each period for a total of 25. "Here are the errors I found on the 25 papers," reports this teacher. "Look over your paper with a fellow student to see if you made the same errors and talk through how to correct it. Change the writing in the computer, so that when I become the referee and grade one paper from all of you, that error is no longer present."

In elementary grades, the conversation is almost exactly the same. There are three fourth grades in this school. All fourth-graders wrote on the same topic. The papers were gathered up, shuffled, and each teacher read five papers. After school yesterday, the three teachers met and tallied the errors from all three fourth grades. Of the 15 papers read, they found 12 made a particular error. The probability is that most students made the same error. "Here are your papers back so you can study to see if you made the same error," they tell their classes. "After three minutes of study, I am going to show you how to avoid this error in future writing. We three teachers had fun after school talking about the best way to teach this to all of you and think what we've come up with will work well. OK, now, take your three minutes to study your paper, either alone or with a classmate."

I hope all the technical errors in my manuscript are caught by editors or me. From past experience I know, however, at least one error will probably slip through. I don't have to like it; the desire is technical perfection. If a reader appreciates this book however, it will be for reasons other than technical. What will impress readers?

Reasoning—the reader admires the logic.

Synthesis—the connecting of various known concepts in a new or unique way.

Divergence—providing the reader alternative ways to
solve problems.

Application—delivering practical concepts the reader can use.

Creativity—appreciation for some portion of the book that seems
particularly clever.

Emotional appeal—the thoughts ring so true the reader is
compelled to act.

So, why am I inserting these thoughts? It is because my advice has focused on the technical aspects of writing. My interest is in helping teachers manage the technical aspects of their profession in a systematic, time-saving manner. Why? So teachers have much more time to coach students with their reasoning, analysis, synthesis, and creativity.

I hope that school board members and superintendents are among the readers of this book. Many of you have board policies requiring far too many grades. I urge you to change the word *grade* to *feedback* in your board policy. Yes, students and their parents should not be in the fog as to how they are progressing. A grade does not help the student know what to do. Feedback provides assistance for improvement. It is very reasonable for each teacher to explain in writing their feedback system to their principal and then to the students and parents. To help board members understand this better, an experiment could be conducted. First, have a former board member who is respected by the current board come to the next six board meetings. At the end of each board meeting have this person give each board member a grade for their performance. If any particular board member wants to know why they received a particular grade, they can call for an appointment. Then for the next six meetings, have this same person provide a written analysis for each board member at the end of the board meeting. The comments will be designed to be helpful, so that the board members can improve. After 12 meetings, the board should be ready to discuss the policy.

I admit that there are teachers in every school district who will not want a change in policy. They use grades as a hammer to control behavior. A change in board policy will not help these poor teachers. So, a policy change could be to change the word *grade* to *feedback or grade*. This change supports the great teachers with coach in every part of their being and will not anger those who see grades as a weapon—thus causing a conflict at the board level.

An objection to what I am writing can legitimately come from the fact that some variation is special. The Iowa teacher that quizzed his algebra students the first part of the school year on seven items randomly selected from the 50 concepts to be known at the end of the year had five statistically special students (Figure 2.10 on page 21). All students answered zero to three correctly except five students. Four had four to five correct and one had six or seven correct. The five demonstrated special variation. In time, most of the students with zero or one correct will progress to two, three, or four correct. (The same format is used weekly to assess progress. A different random seven are selected each week. The questions are variable, but the 50 concepts are constant.) There may be, however, a student or two stuck on zero correct each week. These five students above the system and the couple of students below the system may need their papers checked more often. Remember, there are two kinds of variation: special and common. Common variation is addressed by random selection and improvement of the system as a whole. Special variation needs special attention. Some special attention is to avoid boredom and some special attention is to avoid confusion.

A chapter that describes item analysis and feedback would be incomplete without mentioning the Pareto chart. Clearly, item analysis can be done with tally marks; however, when a more sophisticated analysis is desired, the Pareto chart, Figure 9.1, is the answer. These can be made by students fourth grade and older. The example in Figure 9.1 was made using QI Macros, an add-on to Excel.[8] Not only are the items ranked from most

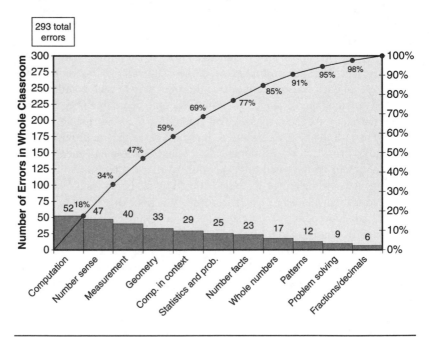

Figure 9.1 A sample Pareto chart.

frequently missed to least frequently missed, but the cumulative percentage is shown. The example shows that 47 percent of the errors were made in computation, number sense, and geometry. This item analysis, for the class as a whole, is to be coupled with individual item analysis completed by students by highlighting their own progress.

CONCLUSION

Teachers should clearly state which activities are for practice with feedback being provided and which activities are to be graded. When the class is studying essential information, such as the mathematics vocabulary on the Washington State Department of Education's Web site, then students are randomly assessed on a portion of the vocabulary to be known at the year's end. When the learning is performance-based, it is students who are randomly selected. Both practices, over time, provide teachers an excellent picture of the learning system without 100 percent inspection. The saved time is for improving the system of learning, for which educators are responsible.

Key Recommendation

Establish distinct periods of time in schools for coaching and other distinct times for being a referee. During coaching times, sample items for informational learning and sample students for performance learning. Provide feedback based upon samples. Reserve 100 percent inspection for referee times.

NO
Inspecting
Judging

YES
Coaching
Learning

10

Teaching Is the Constant; Learning Is the Variable

omework is not a subject. Agriculture, economics, Japanese, mathematics, science, drama, and art are all school subjects; homework is not. Homework is a method to learn the subject. It is a method that is helpful to the majority of students. Nevertheless, it is only a method.

Many teachers have a policy that 40 percent of the grade is based on homework completion. This practice is, in reality, grading the method, and for the minority of students who need a different method to learn, they are doomed to earning a D–, at best. The introduction to this chapter should not be interpreted as anti-homework. The purpose is to help the reader focus on the chapter title. One of the major root causes of educational frustration is treating learning as a variable and teaching as a constant.

It should be the other way around; learning is to be the constant and teaching is to be the variable. Students need to hear from their teachers, "I'm on your case until you learn the content of this course. I'm willing to negotiate teaching; I am unwilling to negotiate learning."

ROOT CAUSE #10

The practice of learning being the variable and teaching being the constant

---

"This simple shift from a focus on teaching to a focus upon learning—has profound implications for schools."[1]

HOMEWORK

Homework policy is a good way to begin this chapter because it raises strong emotions that are a prerequisite to really thinking about learning and teaching. A student should be able to earn an A in any classroom and not complete daily homework. This would entail earning As on all exams and all long-term projects. What is the purpose of daily homework? It is to help students learn the content of the course. Do most students need to complete the daily homework in order to learn the content and earn an A on the exams? Yes. Do all students need to complete the daily homework in order to earn an A on exams? No. We must adjust all grading policies to focus on learning. If you learn this content and if you demonstrate competency on these performance assessments, then the grade will be A. Teachers should clearly state the course expectations the first week of class and do their very best to use methods that create as many winners as possible. Teachers do not know all of the learning methods possible though. Students who take the initiative to learn a different way than what is prescribed must not be penalized because they do not use particular methods to learn.

After sharing these thoughts in an Ohio seminar, an educator relayed to me that the student from her high school with the very highest score on a national science exam received an F in science. Why? Because he didn't complete any daily homework. The message in that classroom clearly was, "It's all about the teaching; learning is only incidental." Educators do not need stories of such malpractice in the newspaper. There is already enough bad news.

Some argue that they must have a policy of homework being 20 percent to 40 percent of the grade because they are teaching responsibility. Who can speak against learning responsibility? My response is that students should be responsible for the learning, not for methods. If some students have a different way of learning something and they learn the expected content, are they being irresponsible? No, they are being responsible. It must be very clear in all classrooms that the focus is on learning.

"I can teach the math, and it is the students' responsibility to learn the way that I teach," is the antithesis of what this chapter is about.[2] Teachers with this attitude will in a few years become quite bitter. If all they think about is teaching, they are actually thinking selfishly. Districts that hire knowledgeable, young, bright, bubbly, selfish teachers are always surprised when in a few years they have middle-aged, grumpy teachers. Selfishness has no choice but to turn into bitterness. It can do nothing else. (I have Vic Cottrell of Ventures for Excellence in Lincoln, Nebraska to thank for this insight.) So it is not only crucial for students that the focus be on learning and not teaching, it is essential for the happiness of the teachers.

When teachers set aside their egos and favorite lesson plans and focus on students meeting standards through a variety of methods, they are much happier people.

A California teacher, who formerly had a policy of homework being 40 percent of the grade, was greatly helped by a student who never turned in homework. By March he had met every standard for the year—both in information and performance. When questioned about never turning in daily homework, he replied, "I'm the oldest of four children and my mom is a single parent. After school I watch my younger brothers and sister until my mother comes home at 8:00. When she comes home, I have better things to do than homework; I'm a kid." Fortunately, this teacher changed her policy because she truly was focused upon learning. Her ego was not tied to her teaching methods, but to students' learning. This student helped her see the error of her policy.

LEARNING IS QUALITY, NOT QUANTITY

My two sons had the incredible experience of having Marion Nordberg in Fullerton, California, for a portion of their primary education in a K–3 combination classroom. One of her many simple reading assignments was to ask students, beginning in kindergarten, "What word do you want to learn to read today?" Marion wrote the word on a flash card and into a booklet entitled "My Important Word Book." Students then wrote (or dictated) sentences to go with the word, wrote the word in their best handwriting, and drew a picture. Any analysis of the word banks collected by students showed that all of the sounds and letters of beginning reading are included in each student's collection. Marion Nordberg demonstrated each day that learning is what is paramount, not teaching. Students learned to read, but not in a predetermined sequence that made sense to adults.

The saying that is passed down from generation to generation of teachers is, "You can lead a horse to water, but you cannot make him drink." This means, "I teach. If you learn the content, great; if you don't—oh well, it's not my fault." Whoever first said that statement should be resurrected and brought to task. That one statement has harmed more students than almost any other educational myth. A more generic way of stating the issue comes from Dobyns and Crawford-Mason. They write, "For public education to improve, the system has to be changed from quantity to quality thinking, and until it is, no number of commission reports or legislative reforms will make it better."[3] Quality and quantity seem to educators like business terms having nothing to do with education. The problem is that educators almost always use different vocabulary than business employees. The quantity term used in education is *cover.* Did you cover the course means, did you teach the content (quantity)? The change Dobyns and Crawford-Mason are suggesting is that the question should be, "Did the students learn the content of the course (quality)?" It doesn't matter if the teacher actually taught it or not; what matters is whether the students learned the content. Learning is about quality.

An example of student learning without teaching comes from an Oregon second grade. The teacher placed a digital clock on a shelf under the analog clock. All year long the students compared the two clocks to see how they both said the same time. At the end of the year, the success rate for reading a clock with the two adjacent clocks was equal to prior years' rates with a couple of weeks of teaching.

WHY TEACHING IS CURRENTLY FOCUS NUMBER ONE

There are several reasons why the focus is on teaching instead of learning. One is that we admire the entertainer-teachers so much. Phil Schlechty says it so well. "If all or nearly all students are to have a high-quality academic experience in school, it is essential that educators redefine the term master teacher to mean a person who is a master at creating engaging work for students and then leading them to do that work. Too often, master teachers today are viewed as persons who are personally engaging, persons who give stellar and entertaining performances, persons who are especially gregarious, and so on."[4]

Jim Collins stated the same concept in a generic way that applies to all professions. He wrote, "The moment a leader allows himself to become the primary reality people worry about, rather than reality being the primary reality, you have a recipe for mediocrity, or worse. This is one of the key reasons why less charismatic leaders often produce better long-term results than their more charismatic counterparts."[5]

A SECOND REASON TEACHING IS FOCUS NUMBER ONE

A second reason teaching is focus number one is that state laws require administrators to evaluate teaching. And the focus is on evaluation of teachers as individuals. Instead, the focus should be on having administrators who can build a team of educators working together to help all students meet the standards for their grade level. Some teachers are best with those students who are struggling, some are best with the overachievers, some are best with reading/language arts, some are best in mathematics, some are geniuses, most are not. Nevertheless, the focus from administration has to be on the learning of students by using the talents of all team members. One way for superintendents to help principals to focus on their team responsibilities is to look at the results of schools by studying the learning of the departing students. In a K–5 school, for example, are the fifth-graders more prepared for middle school than any other prior year? If the second- and third-graders improve, that's wonderful, but the bottom line is, "Are the students prepared for middle school?"

A THIRD REASON TEACHING IS FOCUS NUMBER ONE

A third reason for the focus on teaching is that historically education has not had clear end-of-course expectations. All teachers of algebra I, for example, are allowed to have their own final exam and own course expectations. Now that standards are a normal part of schooling, and these standards are agreed upon and to be used by all, education can make the shift to learning focus. This change should be combined with more "flexibility for teachers."[6] Why? When the school district demands, through evaluation procedures, a focus on teaching, it is very important for teachers to focus on teaching and adhere to dictated practices. If, however, the focus is on learning, teachers should be given much more freedom to help students meet expected standards and pass the district final for the course. This means, at the very least, the homework policy cannot be uniform for all teachers and students. A uniform homework policy means the emphasis is on teaching methods, not on meeting standards. Homework is only one example of the flexibility required for teachers to help all students meet standards. In business, "If workers do not feel they can stop production to fix things that are wrong, they will not report defects."[7] In education, if teachers do not feel they can stop production of lessons to fix learning, they will not take responsibility for failing students.

One way to communicate this change to students is to provide them with a form for alternative assignments. Students are requested to write down long-term assignments from one or more teachers and then to propose an alternative assignment. The students receive permission ahead of time and proceed. For example, a student might have a project due in English, history, and science. He sees how he can combine all three smaller assignments into one huge assignment. He requests permission and learns the content of all three courses with one assignment. It is not unreasonable to expect a student to spend two hours on each of the three projects. However, he might spend 50 hours on the combination of the three. Why the difference? It is because student interest is added to the mix and we all know that personal interest is the key to learning anything. Figure 10.1 is a draft of an alternative assignment form.

SPECIAL EDUCATION

Special education and general education teachers must have this discussion about teaching and learning. I have questioned middle and high school special education teachers from a number of states. The inquiry is merely, how do you spend the majority of your time? The answer is, preparing for individual education plans (IEPs) and helping students with homework. Basically, many secondary special education teachers who have their students for only a portion of the day have become homework clerks. The students bring in their homework from various classes, receive assistance in completing it, and that takes most of the special education time. I've been in the large, urban high school with a dozen or so special education teachers— one for each subject. In these cases, the observation is different; the special education/science teacher is actually teaching science. But in the smaller environments with one or two special education teachers helping all of the students who come to a resource room for a period or two, my observation is true more often than not.

Why is this occurring? It is because the grade in the general education course is 40 percent homework, and special education teachers have no choice but to help their students pass the course. They are trapped. What needs to occur is for general education staff to clearly articulate to students, parents, and special education staff the performance and informational expectations for the year. The special education teacher is then freed up to use a variety of methods to help the students learn the content. Special education students have two teachers working as a team to help them learn the content. When the focus changes from teaching to learning, special education teachers, who have the very most education in alternative learning methods, will be able to utilize their skills.

CONCLUSION

When the focus is changed from teaching to learning, grades will be based on learning. How do we know learning has occurred? It is based on exams and demonstrations. More often than not, learning of information is based on exams and learning of performance expectations (writing, math problem

Permission for Alternative Assignment

_____ *School*

Student(s) _____

Teacher(s) _____

Assignment 1: Teacher _____

Assignment _____

_____

_____

_____

Assignment 2: Teacher _____

Assignment _____

_____

_____

_____

Assignment 3: Teacher _____

Assignment _____

_____

_____

_____

Proposed Alternative Assignment _____

_____

_____

_____

Approval:

_____   _____   _____

Teacher 1   Teacher 2   Teacher 3

Due Date: _____

Figure 10.1 A sample alternative assignment form.

solving, and so on) is based on projects or demonstrations of competence. Peter Senge stated at the National Quality and Education Conference in November 2003 that learning should be about making errors; school is about avoiding mistakes. When the focus changes from teaching to learning and from refereeing to coaching, school personnel can change to a focus that includes learning from errors.

Key Recommendation

Become much more demanding in regard to learning and much more flexible in regard to teaching.

NO
Teaching
Me
YES
Learning
Them

ho

Further Insights

A University-Level Look at the Ten Root Causes of Educational Frustration

Lloyd O. Roettger, PhD

Associate Professor, University of Toledo
Professor Emeritus, University of Central Oklahoma

In today's ever-changing complex society, the development of intellectual capital requires university, teacher, and administrator programs to provide knowledge and competencies in all areas of education that impact schools and successful outcomes for students. The future, one that will be driven by information and knowledge, is dependent on increased prominence of intellectual capital. Intellectual capital is implicated in recent educational, economic, managerial, technological, and sociological developments in a manner previously unknown and largely unforeseen.[1] Whether or not universities can keep pace with the need for intellectual capital in this global information, knowledge-based economy depends on how well they identify and manage the 10 root causes of educational frustration. Lee Jenkins began identifying the root causes of educational frustration in *Improving Student Learning: Applying Deming's Quality Principles in Classrooms.*[2] After reading his book, I attended a national quality education conference where he was a featured speaker. In his presentation, Jenkins outlined the ten root causes of educational frustration and how to reduce or eliminate them. Jenkins's work has been primarily focused on K–12 school settings, but as a university professor I have applied his principles to undergraduate and graduate classrooms and discovered their utility to student success.

Jenkins identified *permission to forget* as the first major educational frustration.[3] The concept of *permission to forget* at the university level at first seemed counterproductive, even unreasonable, since students pay for the teaching and learning they encounter. Simple observation in my own courses, however, revealed that students believed they had permission to forget. They would prepare for exams either by actively studying during the semester or by cramming just before a test. In either case, the student's retention of learned material was fleeting at best. As a professor I was frustrated and concerned that those I was working to prepare as either teachers or school administrators would someday soon walk across a graduation stage only to realize that their hours of class time, studying, and completing assignments had resulted in degree matriculation but not in permanent learning.

My most graphic example of the concept of *permission to forget* was in a graduate educational research class I taught to future school administrators. One of the critical roles of a highly competent school leader is the ability to be an intelligent, active consumer of educational research and translate it for his or her faculty. It is also highly desirable for a school leader to contribute to the field by conducting research on educational interventions, programs, or activities and writing about them. Students always seem to struggle with remembering and using the formatting and writing precepts of the American Psychological Association (APA) as contained in the latest edition of the APA publication manual. All education-related graduate level papers, writing projects, and theses are expected to be written using the latest version of APA style.

As a result, I began to apply continuous improvement principles to the course by developing a list of essential APA facts that clearly defined performance expectations and key skills to be learned. The use of rote memorization of the fact list was never the primary goal. The goal was for students to develop a working knowledge of APA style and to be able to locate and interpret the rules of formatting and writing. All students were given the list at the beginning of the semester and told that there would be a quiz over some of the facts each week. The selection of the test items would be from random sampling from the fact list. Students were told that the goal was to score a 15 out of 15 on the 15th quiz. Their reward would be not taking a final exam over the APA manual. This process randomly tested students over previously taught facts and facts not yet taught. Immediately after taking the weekly quick quiz, the students broke into small groups known as peer review boards to use their APA manuals to find the correct answers and score their papers. As a result, we graphed data showing individual progress, group progress, and the advancement of individual learning within the group immediately after taking the quick quiz. Only group data was displayed in a classroom chart. A benefit was that the system provided real-time feedback about instruction and provided an effective way of communicating progress to students. I once heard it said that feedback, not Wheaties, is the breakfast of champions.

The teaching sequence did not change; I used a set of five simulations for students to follow and produce research proposals and corresponding reports. I have followed this system for 15 classes over eight semesters. Much to my surprise, the process produced some unexpected results. First, as each class of students took the quick quiz week after week they began to take pride in their growth and actually developed an enthusiasm for learning APA style. As Jenkins put it: "Students can and will achieve at higher levels when 'permission to forget' is taken away, data are used to create winners, and kindergarten levels of enthusiasm are restored."[4] Second, the students' use of correct APA style in their simulations significantly improved, so much so that the final reports turned in by the students had 43 percent fewer APA errors.[5] Third, several students were accepted to present their research at regional Educational Research Association conferences and a few even presented at national American Educational Research Association (AERA) conferences. Finally, over 20 percent more students decided to pursue post-masters terminal degrees.

The same benefits of applying continuous improvement principles to K–12 learning identified by Jenkins apply to the university level:[6]

- It focuses the learning by making it explicit.

- It defines for the professor and student what is supposed to be learned during the semester.

- The professor can observe the data and respond with appropriate changes in instruction. The graphs are also useful in giving specific, immediate feedback to students.

- Students take more responsibility for their own learning.

- Students know what they are supposed to be learning, they know at any point in time how they are doing, and how they are doing compared with others.

- They are not given permission to forget.

I have now applied this process to my other classes. It works just as well in undergraduate teacher preparation courses and graduate administrator preparation courses as it has in my research courses. As a senior faculty member and former department chair, I have had the opportunity to teach the process to junior faculty members. Each of them has indicated that the end of semester rating by their students has improved. The educational frustration of students taking or receiving permission to forget is mediated at the university level by applying Jenkins's principles of continuous improvement. When students learn and retain at a high level, the development of intellectual capital becomes easier.

I will avoid rehashing the principles of the other nine root causes since Jenkins has so eloquently explained each in the chapters of this book. I will simply provide the reader with a look at how each root cause has created educational frustration at the university level and briefly investigate its impact.

The second root cause of educational frustration is known as *the wrong statistics*. Jenkins conjectures that education patterned its statistics after athletics, whose aim is to have one and only one winner, and that ranking keeps education from creating as many winners as possible. The ranking of children at the K–12 level is a long-established part of the system at the moment, but it is alien to learning, because it takes the focus away from true learning, which is usually done best by sharing, interacting, exclaiming joyfully at beauty and surprise, facing challenges with fellow learners, and helping each other to learn. Ranking children often has the effect of isolating children from each other. An aside is that testing, as we have it, has become a profitable racket—ranking children through abstract measures with no verifiable connection to character traits we hope to cultivate in children or any connection with developing their mental powers as critical thinkers or only limited connection to locally developed curriculum. No child left untested means all children are ranked. Perhaps educators should spend less time ranking children and more time helping them.

At the university level, each and every course is a competition among students for the highest ranking. I would surmise that every seasoned university faculty member has been approached by students trying to influence their ranking in class. The range of attempts to win "points" with the professor is seemingly endless. Ranking such wonderfully different and talented students against one another misrepresents the student's abilities and efforts, misleads students about the importance of grades, and, most importantly, can hurt young people. Ranking is a *de facto* labeling of a vulnerable group of learners and is inherently wrong. One of the goals of a university must be to create a rich intellectual environment where students are at the center of their own learning. This environment should bring many learners into the winner's circle, not just a few that managed to somehow get a top ranking. The ranking of students encourages a destructive competitiveness and oftentimes leads institutions away from offering students the choice of rich alternatives and toward a useless or ineffectual sameness. It is a disservice to the students and the academy, and, therefore, to our society.

My experience at the university level has involved embracing a variety of ideas, most of which somehow resulted in ranking student performances to encourage competition. None of these ideas eliminated the educational frustration of some students coasting through classes or others slipping through loopholes or cracks in the system. What has made the most difference is abandoning the ranking and competition schemes and following the principles of continuous improvement. This system involves identifying the outcomes of significance that make up the desired learning for the course; translating that into essential facts and concepts that are given to the students with the syllabus on the first day of class; previewing and reviewing the content, concepts, and facts necessary for the student to know and to be considered learned and successful in the class; continuously and randomly assessing students over the essential facts; assisting students in graphing both individual data for personal growth and group data for classwide improvement; and placing class run charts in the classroom to represent the totals of *all* students as a group. This has resulted in the classes working to reach their best score for the year as a class, and students banding together to encourage and even help each other for the good of the group. The process has created more winners in the winners circle.

The third root cause of educational frustration is simply known as the *pendulum.* I have watched the educational pendulum swing back and forth for years. What I have seen over and over is opposing sides fighting for everyone to see the issues from their point of view. Sometimes the pendulum swings to the detriment of students. Allow me to give you a snapshot of how it works at the university level. First, some problem (campuswide or course-isolated) is identified. For example, campus security is breached when a first floor dorm room is broken into from the outside. The result is to move all residence hall occupants to rooms on the higher floors and leave vacant the rooms on the first floor. The follow-up pendulum swing is an architectural trend toward no first-floor dorm rooms. Other university examples of the pendulum swing occur when society's problems become the basis for politically correct university coursework. The University of Chicago offers "Fat Boys: Introduction to Literature and Medicine." This course focuses on obesity and masculinity in the Western tradition. Recommended reading includes Shakespeare plays featuring Falstaff as well as Rabelais' *Gargantua.* The University of Pennsylvania teaches "Vampires: The Undead," which explores the persistence of the image of vampires in literature and film, emphasizing "their metaphoric deftness and adaptability as cultural couriers." At Sacramento State University, although not a pornography class per se, an upper division psychology class requires students to watch sexually explicit films. At the far end of the pendulum swing, academia seems to embrace its own future shock.

On the other hand, if a student's exam scores are not meeting the standards we would like, then do we look at ways of improving the current practice? Do we keep what is good and try to improve on areas of concern?

No, the pendulum swings the other way and we just throw everything out. Any textbooks we were using, teaching methods we found effective, and ways we have learned to teach must be replaced. We must change everything we are doing.

At the public school K–12 level, we even get new legislation to cause changes in our processes and practices. Then we get the string of professors and educational entrepreneurs who, through research or salesmanship, let us know what must be done to improve the teaching of any subjects in which students were found deficient by some standardized test. Then it is up to the school district leaders and school boards to make sure the new and enlightening methods reach the teachers in the schools. New programs are created and in-services developed for teachers and the new programs get implemented. Educational bliss ensues for a brief time before the results of the new and improved programs to teach the subject(s) are assessed. But alas, the programs prove to be just another change and not an improvement. So just when we think we have the problem solved, the educational pendulum swings back the other way, and we are back to throwing out the proverbial baby with the bath water.

At the university level, we have refined the process and engaged in the forensics of debate to justify our research. Ironically the research starts the swinging of another pendulum, which, in turn, leads to another. Allow me to illustrate the multiple pendulums of higher education. First, the problem identification phase reveals the debate about whether theoretical knowledge or practical application ability should be the goal. When the pendulum reaches the top of its arc in one direction, we produce graduates who are prepared to extend their learning through theoretical investigations and classic research studies. Graduates produced at the opposite arc end up with only the practical knowledge that serves them to practice their craft and to earn a living. Hence, we tend to create people who are either so scholarly minded that they are no earthly good or people unprepared to contribute to the global knowledge of society by producing new ideas and relevant data. When this happens do we look at ways of improving the current practice? Do we keep what is good and try to improve upon areas of concern? No, like K–12 schools, the pendulum swings the other way and we just throw everything out. Of course the debates are fueled by the rhetoric of academic freedom and production of research. The research drives its own pendulum and swings to research for promotion and tenure, or research for economic development. Again, both swings of the research pendulum drive the swing of yet other pendulums. The research for promotion and tenure pendulum results in the knowledge needed to let us know what must be done to improve the teaching of either theoretical or practical knowledge, and results in the reversing of the pendulums' swing or in personal recognition for the researcher, which leads to greater security and income, thus affecting yet another pendulum. The research for economic development results in the creation of products or services needed to use in the pursuit of theoretical knowledge or in the application of practical knowledge, and also results in revenues that swing the pendulums of donor giving and university growth, thus reversing the original pendulums' swing. Caught in the middle of all this is the student. Course offerings, class size, professor teaching assignments, supplemental fees, and tuition costs are driven by the pendulum swings.

The fourth of Jenkins's ten root causes is *pressure versus removing barriers*. Jenkins sums up this frustration by concluding that the status quo is maintained by having the pressure to change equalized by the resistance to change.

At the university level, this translates as educational bureaucracy and the ever so slow grinding of the millstone of progress to avoid any shift in the status quo. Presidents, provosts, deans, and department chairs have experienced the resistance added by the faculty when they apply the pressure to change. Hence when those in a position of power add pressure, those not in a position of power add resistance, just as Jenkins says. One might argue that this provides a balance of power, but what really occurs is further stagnation of improvement and the maintenance of the status quo. Argon states "the status quo is unsustainable and . . . a proper debate has yet to take place on reforming (in the proper sense of improving) an ailing public university system."[7] If the senior leadership at the university removes the barriers that are causing professors to add resistance, a much more energetic agenda for innovation could be advanced.

Likewise, if the professor would remove the barriers developed to put pressure on the students whenever possible, the intellectual environment would be enriched. When this occurs, students can be placed at the center of their own learning and their learning can be characterized by choice. An example from my experience is the use of the Internet and other technology to change the way students are taught. Web-assisted teaching and distance learning has allowed my students access to courses and learning without requiring endless hours of seat time. Students can now work and learn at the pace best for them, and they can do it on a schedule that fits their lives rather than a university class schedule. Additional benefits are evident for students, professors, and universities in many other areas. Challenging the status quo by removing barriers, instead of attempting to put more and more pressure on the individual, will lead to finding solutions, instilling hope, and creating the intellectual capital needed to fuel the global knowledge and information society of tomorrow.

The next root cause of educational frustration, *change after change with no improvement,* seems particularly relevant to the university level. It is not uncommon to have a president, a provost, and a vice president of operations pursue different changes to accomplish the same improvement. At first blush this may not sound like a problem, but when the fundamental beliefs driving each change process are at odds with one another, the sum of the changes do not make an improvement. There are many examples of changes that have been implemented in higher education that have not resulted in improvement. One example, from my experience, involved the restructuring of a college to reduce the size of departments by expanding the number of departments, which was pushed through by a new dean. This was more a demonstration of power than a solution to any problem. The dean was certain the faculty would be easier for her to manage and students would get better service. The restructuring occurred and the dean beamed with satisfaction. No data were gathered to evaluate the extent of the improvement, if any. Students became increasingly dissatisfied with the increase in paperwork and bureaucracy that resulted. The climate of the unit worsened, as evidenced by faculty members' complaints among themselves. When approached, the dean denied any problems existed and refused to gather any data about the issue. As a result, the faculty senate decided to collect data by using a questionnaire. The results were overwhelmingly unfavorable for the dean, but she maintained that the change had resulted in an improvement. Further review of the institutional data revealed a rapid decline in enrollment in the college and an exodus of senior faculty members. A visit from the National Council for the Accreditation of Teacher Education (NCATE) resulted in a deficiency in leadership by the dean. The dean still maintained the change was effective and somehow managed to convince the provost that a grumbling faculty member was a happy faculty member. What we had was a classic example of *change, but no improvement*: we experienced change that didn't result in improvement, and we knew nothing improved.

To use data to determine if the change is needed or if the change is producing results is the only way to avoid change-for-change's-sake. We should continue collecting and evaluating the data to see if the changes are bringing improvement. Additionally, changes should be implemented only when the data indicate they are necessary. At the university level, we have enough cynicism and skepticism to hear a hew and cry of "Been there, done that, got the T-shirt, and burned it."

The false belief that experience is the best teacher is the sixth root cause of educational frustration. The accepted, but untested, hypothesis is that our very best teacher is experience. W. Edwards Deming said, "If experience were our best teacher, we'd have no more problems."[8] One would think that organizations, like universities, would learn from their mistakes and never repeat them; however, many university-level mistakes involve large money-management issues. A quick Internet search produces numerous examples. The headlines include: "Because of university errors in computing certain payment rates, four health maintenance organizations were overpaid about $2.8 million"; "University accounting mistakes resulted in $1.1 million overpayment of the faculty health care provider"; "Bookkeeping errors at the university will cost an additional $2.4 million"; "Medical Flexfunds are a bad idea, the university to pick up $600,000 tab"; and "The majority of the problems have been university errors with the accounting system and not with vendors." If experience was the best teacher, we could have saved millions. I could cite examples of the lack of learning from experience with mistakes in the catalog, mistakes in grading, mistakes in registration, errors in computing certain invoices or tuition costs, and so on. Perhaps Jackie "Moms" Mabley's famous quip "if you continue to do what you've always done, you'll always get what you always got" sums up the idea of experience being the best teacher.[9]

The one thing that experience as the best teacher can provide educators is early lessons showing us that we need to work on building expertise. While I believe experience can sometimes be valuable, it seldom if ever leads to expertise. My father used to regularly point out that it was *perfect* practice that led to perfection, not simply practice. Expertise is most easily gained by testing out theories regarding how to improve under the direction of a quality mentor. I am convinced that an addicted student who has pursued education and tested its theories with something akin to fanaticism will prove to be the most useful, most successful, and most valued.

The next root cause of educational frustration is known as *no clear aim*. This is one place where the frustration is nearly the same for both the K–12 and university levels. The lack of clarity of focus in curriculum, teaching goals, learning goals, mission, vision, and philosophy creates frustration for everyone.[10] Students, parents, educators, and patrons of the system view the lack of a clear aim as a weakness in the system. One could think that the university, with its course syllabi, program, and departmental and learned society standards would be focused on and driven toward a clear aim. Unfortunately, that is not the case. I have served on numerous academic affairs committees and grade appeal committees and almost always the student's grievance centers around the professor's confusing grading practices or unclear expectations.

On a personal note, many years ago I was asked to teach a new course, one for which I was not particularly well suited. After giving my class a somewhat generic syllabus and esoterically rambling about the topics within the course, a retired Air Force colonel pointedly asked, "Just what is the aim of this course?" I was suddenly faced with the realization that I had no clear aim. The course proved to be the worst I ever taught, as evidenced by my students' course evaluations. Later in my career, as a department chair, I created a professional development program to help my faculty create specific syllabi with clearly defined aims—the result was happier students and successfully promoted and tenured faculty.

Poor psychology, educational frustration root cause number eight, tells us that it is not our responsibility to motivate the students. In university teacher preparation programs, we teach future teachers the motivation acronym FLIKRS and tell them that when student motivation flickers, they should use the tools of feeling tone, level of concern, interest, knowledge of results, rewards, and success. We teach them the five steps of building student self-esteem, the use of positive self-talk, the use of logical consequences, and a handful of other motivation techniques. This entire imposed curriculum sends the message that the teacher's sole responsibility, and, at times, their only purpose is to motivate students. But it is not our responsibility to motivate them; they were born motivated and entered kindergarten motivated to learn. It is our responsibility to cause learning to happen. In my opinion, if learning doesn't happen, teaching didn't occur. It appears that the poor psychology practiced at the K–12 level has been parented at the university level. I realize that my colleagues in the education psychology department would likely take issue with these thoughts, but I wonder how much research effort has gone into determining why the motivation to learn wanes as the child experiences more and more of the motivation techniques we so effectively teach future teachers.

At the university level, the poor psychology mistakes are not the same as those made in K–12 settings. Yes, we try most of the motivation techniques of elementary and secondary school teachers and usually with limited success. Among the poor psychology practices of higher education is assuming every student is in class to soak up the vast amounts of wisdom you intend to dispense. It seems to make sense because they have selected your course, paid their money, and appeared in the classroom. But perhaps the most vivid example of poor psychology at the university level is our failure to recognize the characteristics and demographics of the adult learner and then to use that information to effectively teach our students.[11] We can avoid the educational frustration of poor psychology by using the characteristics of our audience to plan. The plans should include self-directed activities, independent projects, and group work. We should provide support, structure, practical hints, and variety.[12] We also need to remember that our audience is mature and independent. Therefore, no lines in the sand.

The ninth root cause for educational frustration presented by Jenkins is known as *always the referee, rarely the coach.* He points out that typically the teacher works with the students as both coach and referee from day one. The process of being the referee and the coach seems to be the accepted standard at the university level. In fact, being the referee has become more accepted than being a coach. A student's first question in most classes reflects concern about how they will be evaluated; hence the referee's role is escalated. A university syllabus would be considered incomplete without a detailed explanation of how grades are determined, however, there is no real expectation of the syllabus including a listing of the essential facts and concepts students are expected to learn; hence the referee's role is again escalated. In my experience, students are surprised by my offers to coach them to success on assignments and projects. Students sometimes look at me with wonder when I freely give them my home and cell phone numbers. They are even more amazed when I suggest that when they need some coaching, a call would be appropriate. I know the concept of coaching a student has gone from some of my colleagues' teaching repertoires when I hear comments like "I've just created an exam no one can ace!" The concept of knowledge and how to measure it will continue to be a debate at every level of the educational system, as will the dilemma that educators face when trying to coach and referee the same learning activity.

In the last of the ten root causes, *teaching is the constant; learning is the variable,* Jenkins aptly points out that teaching is the constant in classrooms and learning is the variable. He goes on to say that learning should be the constant and teaching the variable. He laments that we say "you can lead a horse to water, but cannot make him drink," which means I teach but have little impact upon learning. My thoughts are that perhaps we should salt the horses' oats or extend the time between offers of water. But alas we are not educating horses. There is some merit in both time and seasoning in the education of our students. For learning to become the variable, time must also become a variable. Is it so important when a student learns a concept, or whether he or she learns the concept? For decades in education we have used the speed at which a student learns to sort and slot them in our classes. For example, if we teach a difficult concept and on Tuesday student W gets it, on Wednesday student X gets it, on Thursday student Y gets it, on Friday we test, and finally, on Monday, student Z gets it; the sorting and slotting occurs by awarding W an A, X a B, Y a C, and Z gets to retake the class next year! Z learned the same concepts as W did, but the learning was not valued or rewarded. Again I ask, is it more important *when* a student learns or *whether* a student learns? Therefore, if learning is to become the constant, then time must be allowed to be a variable.

At the university level, the linkage between teaching, learning, and time is just as frustrating as in K–12. Students are on a fast track, they have busy lives with numerous activities and responsibilities, and each class is taught as if it were their only class. Many university professors are content experts with little or no pedagogical skills. The result is sometimes poor teaching driven by an absolute timeline with whatever learning that occurs as a by-product. I don't say this as an indictment of the university or any of my learned colleagues. Rather, it is a systems problem. The constant is the teaching; I know this because the closure of every lesson, class, or course happens on a time schedule and not necessarily in the minds of the learners.

Learning is expected at the university, even taken for granted. But how often do we hear graduates express their fears that they didn't learn enough by graduation to be successful? Those graduates are the ones we send forth to create the intellectual capital necessary to fuel the global knowledge society that lies before us. Universities should consider mapping the development of intellectual capital in its graduates. Mapping intellectual capital development is a task that empirically investigates the influence of teaching on knowledge creation and the relationships between teaching, learning, and time.

Appendix A
What Is Root Cause Analysis?

A t least a dozen books exist that describe how to conduct root cause analysis. One can become an expert in this process alone because there are so many insights to be gained by organizations and their leaders. *Permission to Forget: And Nine Other Root Causes of America's Frustration with Education* does not attempt to rewrite or compete with the excellent titles already available on the techniques of root cause analysis.

This short appendix is written to give the reader a little deeper understanding of the definitions and process. John Dew wrote, "Root cause analysis is a structured questioning process that enables people to recognize and discuss the underlying beliefs and practices that result in poor quality in an organization. A root cause is a basic causal factor, which if corrected or removed will prevent recurrence of a situation."[1]

He further wrote, "What some practitioners are reluctant to admit is that root causes reside in the values and beliefs of an organization. Until the analysis moves to this level, an organization has not begun to grapple with root causes. An appropriate rule of thumb for knowing how deep to dig in conducting a root cause analysis is to dig until you reach the point of admitting something really embarrassing about the organization, but don't go so far that you are in the field of theology."[2]

Dave Nelson wrote, "A why–why diagram says, 'Slow down. Before we find a solution, let's find the root cause.' A team using this approach begins with a problem and relentlessly asks why until the root cause or causes, not just the obvious cause, are found. Every answer turns into another question, and the exercise continues until the team cannot reasonably ask why anymore."[3]

A graphic that can be used for root cause analysis is the tree diagram. Begin with one question and several answers are discovered. Each answer becomes a branch of the tree with its own why question. Then, when these secondary questions are answered, even more branches may appear. In my sample analysis, I ask, "Why does America have such frustration with its education system." I discovered four answers:

1. Students are apathetic.

2. Students don't remember content taught in prior grades.

3. All of the changes that have occurred in education don't seem to have helped.

4. It seems employees are not doing their best.

Each of these four main branches then is divided into other branches with even more branches.

Dean Gano would have us ask *why* like a three-year-old who never stops after one or two questions. People performing root cause analysis need to keep on asking why.

Appendix B is my sample root cause analysis. The root causes at the end of each series of whys are the chapters of this book.

Appendix B
The Search for the Root Causes

Question: *Why* is America frustrated with education?

Answer: Students forget what they were taught in prior grades and time is wasted reteaching it.

Question: *Why* did students forget what they were taught?

Answer: They never really learned it in the first place.

Question: *Why* didn't they learn it in the first place?

Answer: They crammed.

Question: *Why* did they cram?

Answer: They needed a grade or a 100%.

Question: *Why* is the grade so important?

Answer: People falsely believe grades equal learning.

Question: *Why* do people equate grades and learning?

Answer: They have no understanding of how to base grades on long-term memory rather than on short-term memory.

Question: *Why* is America frustrated with education?

Answer: Students are apathetic.

Question: *Why* are so many students apathetic?

Answer: They received the message that they didn't quite have what it takes to be successful.

Question: *Why* did they receive this message?

Answer: Normal data systems caused public humiliation.

Question: *Why* are data used to discourage so many?

Answer: Educators have been convinced grades must match the bell curve.

Question: *Why* do educators use the bell curve?

Answer: There is no knowledge that educators' desire to create as many winners as possible is being undermined by ill-advised adoption of athletic statistics.

Question: *Why* is America frustrated with education?

Answer: Students are apathetic.

Question: *Why* are so many students apathetic?

Answer: They gradually lost the enthusiasm they had in kindergarten.

Question: *Why* have they lost their enthusiasm?

Answer: Students seem to no longer care about school.

Question: *Why* don't they care any more?

Answer: Incentives that used to work, no longer work.

Question: *Why* don't incentives work?

Answer: After hundreds of incentives, all intrinsic motivation for school work is gone.

Question: *Why* is instrinsic motivation gone?

Answer: They are normal kids and the system uses poor educational psychology.

Question: *Why* is America frustrated with education?

Answer: Students don't want to do the work.

Question: *Why* don't students want to do the work?

Answer: They are bored.

Question: *Why* are they bored?

Answer: They are not learning from assigned work.

Question: *Why* aren't students learning from assigned work?

Answer: There are too many normal kids who want to learn their own way.

Question: *Why* cannot kids learn their own way?

Answer: Focus is based on teaching, not on learning.

Question *Why* is the focus based on teaching and not on learning?

Answer: State laws require that teachers be evaluated on teaching, not on learning.

Question: *Why* is America frustrated with education?

Answer: Nothing seems to get better.

Question: *Why* does nothing seem to get better?

Answer: It is true: "Been there; done that."

Question: *Why* do educators say, "Been there; done that."

Answer: Each change only lasts a few years, if that long.

Question: *Why* only a short time?

Answer: The educational pendulum swings from focus on basics to focus on deeper understanding to focus on basics back to deeper understanding, and so on.

Question: *Why* this pendulum?

Answer: Educators push for deeper understanding and the public pushes for basics.

Question: *Why* this difference of opinion?

Answer: Neither group believes schools can excel in both.

Question: *Why* not both?

Answer: Too much content for both basics and deeper understanding.

Question: *Why* too much?

Answer: Basics are full of trivia.

Question: *Why* is America frustrated with education?

Answer: The last five changes improved nothing.

Question: *Why* no improvement?

Answer: There are no baseline data. Educators don't really know for sure if the change improved anything or not.

Question: *Why* are there no baseline data?

Answer: In a big hurry to make the change.

Question: *Why* in a big hurry?

Answer. There is no understanding of rule one in change, which is, determine how we will know if the change actually results in improvement.

Question: *Why* are we missing this understanding?

Answer: The focus is on leverage, not on teamwork.

Question: *Why* leverage?

Answer: Leaders are taught to blame people and not how to improve the system.

Question: *Why* is America frustrated with education?

Answer: Employees are not doing their best.

Question: *Why* are employees not doing their best?

Answer: They have too much to do.

Question: *Why* do employees have too much to do?

Answer: Bosses keep piling it on.

Question: *Why* do bosses keep piling it on?

Answer: Their bosses keep piling it on.

Question: *Why* do the top bosses keep piling it on?

Answer: Bosses don't know their job is to remove barriers.

Question: *Why* don't they know this?

Answer: They never ever heard a boss say, "What barriers can I remove to help you to do your very best?"

Question: *Why* is America frustrated with education?

Answer: Employees believe they are doing their best now and can do no better.

Question: *Why* do employees believe they can do no better?

Answer: Their experience tells them so.

Question: *Why* do they rely so much on experience?

Answer: They have been taught from childhood that experience is the best teacher.

Question: *Why* is this belief not challenged?

Answer. Employees lack the knowledge of how easy it is to test theories as a better way to learn.

Question: *Why* is America frustrated with education?

Answer: In spite of best efforts, nothing gets significantly better.

Question: *Why* is nothing getting better in spite of all this hard work?

Answer: Efforts are uncoordinated.

Question: *Why* are efforts uncoordinated?

Answer: Everyone has their own objectives.

Question: *Why* does everyone have their own objectives?

Answer: People rebel at "do it like I tell you" management.

Question: *Why* do managers attempt "do it like I tell you" styles?

Answer: Leaders don't know about the power of a common aim for either students or staff.

Question: *Why* don't leaders know this?

Answer: They have been told management by objectives is ultimate. They don't know fourth generation management (common aim, teamwork) exists.

Question: *Why* is America frustrated with education?

Answer: Teachers are not using data to inform their instruction.

Question: *Why* aren't teachers using data to inform their instruction?

Answer: There's no time for item analysis.

Question: *Why* is there no time for item analysis?

Answer: Spending time on 100 percent inspection.

Question: *Why* so much time on inspection?

Answer: They falsely believe they can inspect quality into student work.

Question: *Why* do educators persist in trusting inspection to improve quality?

Answer: They don't know about or trust sampling techniques that create the time for item analysis.

Question: *Why* don't educators sample to create time for item analysis?

Answer: Statistics, probability, and sampling techniques are taught by math and science teachers for how "the rest of the world works," but are not used in education.

Question: *Why* are these "rest of the world" techniques not used in education?

Answer: I wish I knew! Maybe my two books, the Continuous Improvement Series, and seminars will help.

Appendix C
Key Science Concepts Examples
Jeff Burgard

ASTRONOMY

1. Stars are spinning clouds of gases that radiate heat and light through nuclear fusion reactions, changing hydrogen to helium.

2. Most astronomers believe the big bang theory of the universe, which states that the universe began with a great explosion of concentrated matter and energy and has been expanding ever since.

3. The spectrum of the light coming from a star helps determine its temperature and composition.

4. Our sun is a medium-sized star.

5. Stars are made by the gravitational attraction of the gases in a nebula.

6. Stars have a lifecycle. The way a star dies is determined by its mass.

7. Massive stars can turn into black holes, supernovas, or neutron stars. Smaller stars cool to become white or brown dwarfs.

8. The closest galaxy to our own Milky Way is the Andromeda galaxy.

9. Distances to stars are so great that they are calculated by how far light travels in a year, or "light years." Light travels 300,000 km per second.

10. The distance from earth to the sun is called an astronomical unit (AU).

11. Galaxies are huge collections of billions of stars held together by gravitational attraction.

12. Current theory says that gravitational attraction is caused by a warp in the "space-time continuum."

13. The greater the mass of an object, the greater the gravitational attraction.

14. Escape velocity is the speed a rocket needs to travel to escape the gravitational attraction of a celestial object.

15. Elliptical orbits are caused by the combination of inertia and gravitational attraction of the object being orbited.

16. A solar system contains a star, comets, asteroids, planets, and moons.

17. Period of revolution is when one object travels around another. For a planet, one revolution is one year.

18. Period of rotation is one spin on the axis. For a planet, one rotation is one day.

19. The moon appears to go through phases because of a person's perspective from earth as the moon revolves. One side is always lit, but we can only see part of it depending on its position.

20. The phases of the moon are: new, crescent, first quarter, gibbous, full, gibbous, last quarter, crescent.

21. The seasons are caused by the relationship of the tilt of the earth's axis to its position around the sun.

HEAT

22. Heat is the form of energy that causes the motion of molecules.

23. Cold is the absence of heat.

24. Heat always moves from warmer objects to cooler objects until they reach equilibrium.

25. Temperature is a measurement of the average speed of the molecules within a substance.

26. Conduction is the transfer of heat through a substance by direct contact of the molecules.

27. Convection is the transfer of heat through a substance due to density changes within the substance.

28. Radiation is the transfer of heat through waves.

29. Specific heat is the amount of energy needed to raise 1 gram of a substance one degree Celsius.

30. Zero degrees Celsius is the freezing point of water. One hundred degrees Celsius is the boiling point of water.

31. Zero degrees Kelvin (minus 273 degrees Celsius) is absolute zero, the point where all molecular motion stops.

32. Substances that transfer heat easily are called conductors.

33. Substances that don't transfer heat easily are called insulators.

34. Heating causes most substances to expand. Cooling causes them to contract.

35. A substance exists as a solid, liquid, or gas depending on the motion of its molecules. Fast—gas, medium—liquid, slow—solid.

36. Changes in a substance's state occur when heat energy changes.

37. Freezing point is the temperature at which substances change from liquid to solid. Melting point is from solid to liquid.

38. Boiling point is determined by pressure, not temperature. When the pressure in the substance equals the pressure outside the substance, it boils.

39. Sublimation is when a solid changes directly to a gas.

40. Evaporation occurs when a substance changes from a liquid to a gas. Condensation occurs when a substance changes from a gas to liquid.

GEOLOGY

41. The earth is composed of the core and mantle and is covered with the crust, which is cracked into sections called plates.

42. The plates move because of convection currents in the magma of the earth's mantle.

43. Earthquakes are caused by the sudden movement of part of the earth's crust.

44. Earthquake energy is transferred through surface (S)-waves, pulse (P)-waves, and longitudinal (L)-waves.

45. Faults are cracks in the earth's crust. The four types are strike slip, normal, reverse, and thrust.

46. The focus point is the place along the fault where the earthquake begins.

47. The epicenter of the earthquake is the point on the surface directly above the point where the quake occurred.

48. The Richter scale measures the energy released during an earthquake.

49. Volcanoes are caused by subduction of the earth's crust, which heats, melts, and rises to the earth's surface.

50. Most sedimentary rocks are formed when sediments are deposited, compacted, and cemented.

51. Igneous rocks are formed when magma cools.

52. Slow cooling and evaporation can create large crystals. Fast cooling can make small crystals.

53. Crystals are a result of the repeating bonding patterns of the atoms that the substance is made of.

54. Metamorphic rock is formed when igneous or sedimentary rock is transformed by heat and pressure.

55. Minerals are inorganic, naturally occurring compounds in the earth.

56. Minerals have specific properties: crystal shape, cleavage, hardness, color, luster, streak, and density.

57. The major causes of erosion are water, ice, plants, wind, and gravity.

58. Soils are composed of minerals, microorganisms, and decayed organic matter.

59. The four major volcano types are plug dome, shield, strato, and cinder cone.

60. Fossils provide important evidence of how life and environmental conditions have changed.

CHEMISTRY

61. Atomic number of an atom is the number of protons.

62. Atomic mass, or weight, is the number of protons plus the number of neutrons.

63. An atom is the smallest particle of an element and contains *protons* which are positively charged, *neutrons* which are neutral, and *electrons* which are negatively charged.

64. A stable atom has an equal number of protons and electrons.

65. An ion is a charged atom with an unequal number of protons and electrons.

66. An element is the simplest pure substance.

67. A molecule is made up of two or more atoms.

68. A compound is a pure substance formed by combining two or more elements.

69. Compounds containing specific combinations of elements have identifiable properties and react in predictable ways. (Examples are acids, bases, salts, polymers, alcohols, amino acids, etc.)

70. Combining equal amounts of acid and base particles makes a solution neutral.

71. All matter has *mass* (the amount of matter), *weight, volume* (the space the matter takes up), and *density* (mass divided by volume).

72. Matter can be identified by its physical properties such as color, shape, and texture.

73. Chemical properties are the ways in which a substance reacts with another substance.

74. A physical change has occurred when there is a change in the physical properties, but the chemical properties remain the same.

75. A chemical reaction has occurred when both the physical and the chemical properties have changed.

76. Endothermic reactions have occurred when energy is absorbed and the product is cooler. Exothermic reactions give off heat and make the product warmer.

77. Synthetic materials are not found in nature and are made using our knowledge of chemistry to transform raw substances into materials with desirable properties.

78. Synthetic materials can help reduce the depletion of some natural resources, reduce cost, and create better products.

79. The disposal of synthetic materials can create safety and environmental problems.

80. A solute is a substance that is dissolved in a solution. A solvent does the dissolving in a solution.

81. A solution is a mixture in which one substance is dissolved in another substance.

GENETICS

82. DNA (deoxyribonucleic acid) is the chemical compound that codes all life and is found in the chromosome of each cell.

83. Each species has a specific number of paired chromosomes in the nucleus of each body cell.

84. Genotype is the gene makeup of a specific trait. Phenotype is the physical appearance of a specific trait.

85. Homozygous means having the same genes for a trait. Heterozygous means having different genes for a trait.

86. Dominant traits are the traits that are expressed when one or two of the same are present. Recessive genes seem to disappear when only one of the same genes is present.

87. In codominance and incomplete dominance neither trait is dominant.

88. Genes are segments of DNA found on chromosomes.

89. In sexual reproduction, two parent sex cells, each with half the number of chromosomes, combine to form the offspring.

90. Traits carried on the X chromosome are sex-linked traits.

91. Genetic engineering is the process in which genes or pieces of DNA are transferred from one organism to another.

92. Plants reproduce sexually through pollination and fertilization.

93. A flower is the reproductive structure of the plant.

94. Fertilization occurs when a male sex cell joins a female sex cell.

95. In a flowering plant, the stamen produces the pollen (the male sex cell), and the pistil produces the ovule (the female sex cell).

96. A seed is a fertilized ovule and can be found in fruits, nuts, and pods.

TECHNOLOGY AND SO FORTH

97. Scientific knowledge and development are dependent on technological advances.

98. Technological advances have enabled humans to do complex operations, process large amounts of data quickly, extend our observations, and manufacture intricate devices.

99. Technological development is based on understanding scientific principles, the physical limitations of the materials, and the scope of our knowledge.

100. An *observation* is a record of what you see. An *inference* is a conclusion based on what you observe.

Endnotes

Preface

1. Lloyd Dobyns and Clare Crawford-Mason, *Quality or Else* (Boston: Houghton Mifflin, 1991), 223.
2. Russell L. Ackoff, *The Democratic Organization* (New York: Oxford University Press, 1994), xi.
3. Kathleen Kennedy Manzo, "Teachers Picking Up Tools to Map Instructional Practices," *Education Week* (8 October 2003): 8.

Introduction

1. *The Jefferson Memorial*, Quality Minutes Video Collection, The Juran Institute, Wilton, CT, 1996.
2. Lee Jenkins, *Improving Student Learning: Applying Deming's Quality Principles in Classrooms,* Second Edition (Milwaukee: ASQ Quality Press, 2003).

Chapter 1

1. Lee Jenkins, *Improving Student Learning: Applying Deming's Quality Principles in Classrooms,* Second Edition (Milwaukee: ASQ Quality Press, 2003).
2. Herb Childress, "Seventeen Reasons Why Football Is Better Than High School," *Kappan* (March 1998). www.pdkintl.org/kappan/kchi9804.htm.
3. Ronald A. Wolk, "A Little Humility," *Education Week* 15, no. 2 (2003): 4.
4. Edward L. Deci, *Why We Do What We Do* (New York: Penguin Books, 1995), 48–49.

5. Myron Tribus, "Selected Papers on Quality and Productivity Improvement," *National Society of Professional Engineers:* 21.

6. Kathleen Kerwin, "When Flawless Isn't Enough," *Business Week* (8 December 2003): 82.

7. David Kiley, "US Automakers Increasing Efficiency, Report Says," *USA Today* (19 June 2003): 3B.

8. Tamara Henry, "Kids Get 'Abysmal' Grade in History." *USA Today* (10 May 2002): 1.

9. Joseph M. Juran, *Juran on Quality by Design: The New Steps for Planning Quality into Goods and Services* (New York: Free Press, 1992), 2.

Chapter 2

1. Erika Chavez, "State Releases New Rankings for Schools," *Sacramento Bee* (21 February 2003).

2. Douglas Reeves, *The Leader's Guide to Standards* (San Francisco: Jossey-Bass, 2002), 5.

3. Matthew Boyle, "Performance Reviews: Perilous Curves Ahead," *Fortune* (28 May 2001): 187.

4. "Sophomore Challenges Calculation on Grades," *The Arizona Republic* (29 May 2004): B5.

5. James Fallows, "The Early Decision Racket," *The Atlantic Monthly* (September 2001): 37–52.

6. Christy Watson, "State SAT Scores Lead Region," *The Oklahoman* (29 August 2001): 12A.

7. Dana Tofig, "No Grades on State Report Cards," *The Atlanta Journal-Constitution* (27 February 2003), www.accessatlanta.com/ajc/epaper/editions/thursday/metro_e3d54b96bff154002e.html.

8. John D. Bransford, Ann L. Brown, and Rodney R. Cocking, eds., *How People Learn* (Washington DC: National Academy Press, 1999), 149.

9. Douglas Reeves, *The Leader's Guide to Standards*, (San Francisco: Jossey-Bass, 2002), 18.

10. Howard Kirschenbaum, Sidney Simon, and Rodney Napier, *Wad-Ja-Get?* (New York: Hart Publishing, 1971), 191.

11. Lynn Olson, "Study Relates Cautionary Tale of Misusing Data," *Education Week* (21 May 2003): 12.

12. Jeff Zogg and Bill McCleery, "ISTEP Changes Pose Challenges," *Indystar* (27 February 2003). Indystar.com/print/articles/2/025564-5352-009.html.

13. Michelle Galley, "More Errors Are Seen In the Scoring of Tests, Boston Researchers Say," *Education Week* (18 June 2003): 10.

14. Rudolph Giuliani, *Leadership* (New York: Hyperion, 2002).

15. Ibid., 72.

16. Ibid., 74.

17. Ibid., 167.
18. Ibid., 96.
19. W. Edwards Deming, *Schools and Communities Cooperating for Quality—Lessons for Learners* (Alexandria, VA: American Association of School Administrators), ch. 2, p. 9.
20. Edward L. Deci, *Why We Do What We Do* (New York: Penguin Books, 1996), 155.
21. Reeves, *The Leader's Guide to Standards,* 99.
22. W. Edwards Deming, *The New Economics* (Cambridge, MA: Massachusetts Institute of Technology, 1994), 98–99.
23. Ibid.
24. Lynne Hare, "SPC: From Chaos to Wiping the Floor," *Quality Digest* (July 2003): 58.
25. See *Total Quality Tools for Educators,* PQ Systems, for directions and QI Macros for an add-on to Excel for creating the actual charts.
26. Pedro A. Noguera, "Transforming High Schools," *Educational Reading* (May 2004): 28.
27. Michelle Galley, "Texas Principal Posts Test Scores of Classes," *Education Week* (17 September 2003): 3.
28. Norman Draper and Allie Shah, "Report Cards on Schools Issued," *Star Tribune* (22 August 2003): 1.
29. Deming, *The New Economics,* 27.

Chapter 3

1. Ann Bradley, "McGuffey Eclectic Readers First Published in 1836, Still Sell 100,000 Copies a Year of 1879 Edition," *Education Week* (2 October 2002): 3.
2. Louise Matteoni, Wilson H. Lane, Floyd Sucher, and Versie G. Burns, *Maybe a Mile* (Oklahoma City: The Economy Company, 1972).
3. Kathleen Kennedy Manzo, "N.Y.C. Hangs Tough Over Maverick Curriculum," *Education Week* (15 October 2003): 1.
4. Michael Clay Thompson, *Classics in the Classroom* (Unionville, NY: Royal Fireworks Press, 1995), 48.
5. John D. Bransford, Ann L. Brown, and Rodney R. Cocking, eds., *How People Learn* (Washington DC: National Academy Press, 1999), 117.
6. Douglas Reeves, *The Leader's Guide to Standards* (San Francisco, Jossey-Bass, 2002), 12.
7. Bransford, Brown, and Cocking, *How People Learn,* 19.
8. Michael Clay Thompson, *Classics in the Classroom* (Unionville, NY: Royal Fireworks Press, 1995), 48.
9. Catherine Gewertz, "City Districts Embracing K–8 Schools," *Education Week* (19 May 2004).

Chapter 4

1. Edward Deci, *Why We Do What We Do* (New York: Penguin Books, 1995), 1.
2. W. Edwards Deming, *The New Economics* (Cambridge, MA: MIT Press, 1993), 33.
3. Kelly Arey, "When Standardization Replaces Innovation," *Education Week* (8 May 2002): 32.
4. Richard Elmore, *Building a New Structure for School Leadership* (Washington, DC: The Albert Shanker Institute, 2000), 27.
5. Pedro A. Noguera, "Transforming High Schools," *Educational Leadership* (May 2004): 30.
6. Joseph DeStefano and Ellen Foley, "The Human-Resource Factor," *Education Week* (16 April 2003): 44.
7. Results, April, 2003, National Staff Development Council, Oxford, OH, p. 4.
8. Martha Raffaele, "PA Parents May Get Own Report Cards," *The Arizona Republic* (7 February 2003): 8.
9. Peter Senge, "Leading Learning Organizations" in *The Leader of the Future*, eds. Marshall Goldsmith and Francis Hesselbein (San Francisco: Jossey-Bass, 1996), 2.
10. Deci, *Why We Do What We Do*, 2, 9.
11. Peter Senge, *The Fifth Discipline* (New York: Doubleday, 1990), 225.
12. Deci, *Why We Do What We Do*, 142.
13. Mary Walton, *The Deming Management Method* (New York: Putnam Publishing Group, 1986), 70.
14. Results, March, 2003, National Staff Development Council, Oxford, OH, p. 4.
15. Deci, *Why We Do What We Do*, 42.
16. Jim Collins, *Good to Great* (New York: HarperCollins, 2001), 75.
17. W. Edwards Deming, *Schools and Communities Cooperating for Quality— Lessons for Leaders* (Washington, DC: American Association of School Administrators, 1992), ch. 6, pg. 6.
18. Karen Bemowski, "Leaders on Leadership," *Quality Progress* (January 1996): 44.
19. Bernard M. Bass, *Leadership, Psychology and Organizational Behavior* (New York: Harper and Brothers, 1960), 123.
20. William Glasser, *The Quality School* (New York: Harper and Row, 1990), 7.
21. William Scherkenbach, *Deming's Road to Continual Improvement* (Knoxville, TN: SPC Press, 1991), 293.
22. Warren Bennis, *Why Leaders Can't Lead* (San Francisco: Jossey-Bass, 1989), 14.
23. Douglas Reeves, *Leader's Guide to Standards* (San Francisco: Jossey-Bass, 2001).
24. Robert Marzano, *What Works in Schools: Translating Research into Action* (Alexandria, VA: ASCD, 2002), 48.
25. Ibid., 127–129.
26. Ibid., 118.

27. Jeff Burgard, *Continuous Improvement in the Science Classroom* (Milwaukee: ASQ Quality Press, 2000).
28. Reeves, *Leader's Guide to Standards,* 50.

Chapter 5

1. Peter Senge, "Leading Learning Organizations" in *The Leader of the Future,* eds. Marshall Goldsmith and Francis Hesselbein (San Francisco: Jossey Bass, 1996), 2.
2. William Scherkenbach, *Deming's Road to Continual Improvement* (Knoxville, TN: SPC Press, 1991), 109.
3. W. Edwards Deming, *The New Economics* (Cambridge, MA: MIT Press, 1993), 38.
4. Jim Collins, *Good to Great* (New York: HarperCollins, 2001), 69, 172.
5. Pedro A. Noguera, "Transforming High Schools," *Educational Leadership* (May 2004): 29.
6. Nancy C. Rodriquez, "School Schedule Has Little Effect on Test Scores," *The Courier-Journal* (3 March 2003).
7. Gene Koretz, "Teacher Tests Fail the Grade," *Business Week* (24 November 2003): 28.
8. Phillip C. Schlechty, presentation in Boise, Idaho, November 1, 1999.
9. Richard Elmore, *Building a New Structure for School Leadership* (Washington, DC: The Albert Shanker Institute, 2001), 12.
10. Pat Kossen, "Lax Data Skew Rate of State's Dropouts," *The Arizona Republic* (29 May 2004): B1.
11. Debra Viadero and Erik W. Robelen, "Research Research," *Education Week* (13 February 2002): 30.
12. Myron Tribus, "Quality and Education According to the Teachings of Deming and Feurestein." www.mehs.edu.state.ak.US/quality/demingfuerenstein.pdf.
13. John G. Conyers and Robert Ewy, *Charting Your Course* (Milwaukee: ASQ Quality Press, 2004), 96–97.
14. Elmore, *Building a New Structure for School Leadership,* 13.
15. W. Edwards Deming, *Schools and Communities Cooperating for Quality— Lessons for Leaders* (Arlington, VA: American Association of School Administrators, 1990), ch. 6, p. 6.
16. Myron Tribus, "Selected Papers on Quality and Productivity Improvement," (paper presented at National Society of Professional Engineers, Washington, DC), 13.
17. Deming, *Schools and Communities Cooperating for Quality—Lessons for Leaders,* ch. 6, p. 2.

Chapter 6

1. Dale Carnegie, *How to Win Friends and Influence People* (New York: Simon and Schuster, 1936), xxiv.

2. Mike Schmoker, "Planning for Failure?" *Education Week* (12 February 2003): 39.
3. Rudolph Giuliani, *Leadership* (New York: Hyperion, 2002), 310.
4. John Merrow, "Try Something Different for Weak Students," *USA Today* (15 April 2002): 13A.
5. Giuliani, *Leadership*, 158.
6. *The Fifth Discipline* (New York: Doubleday, 1990), 277.
7. Janet Sugameli, "Night School Works Best for Some Students," *The Detroit News* (10 March 2003), www.detnews.com/2003/schools/0303/10/d05-104055.htm.
8. John G. Conyers and Robert Ewy, *Charting Your Course* (Milwaukee: ASQ Quality Press, 2004), 110.
9. Susan Leddick et al., *Total Quality Tools for Education (K–12)* (Dayton, OH: PQ Systems, 1998).

Chapter 7

1. Richard Elmore, *Building a New Structure for School Leadership* (Washington, DC: The Albert Shanker Institute, 2000), 25.
2. John G. Conyers and Robert Ewy, *Charting Your Course* (Milwaukee: ASQ Quality Press, 2004), 3.
3. Rudulph Giuliani, *Leadership* (New York: Hyperion, 2002), 73, 175, 301.
4. W. Edwards Deming. *The New Economics* (Cambridge, MA: MIT, 1994), 73.
5. Russell Ackoff, *The Democratic Organization* (New York: Oxford University Press, 1994), 30.
6. Douglas Reeves, *The Leader's Guide to Standards* (San Francisco: Jossey-Bass, 2002), 10.
7. Robert Marzano, *What Works in Schools* (Alexandra, VA: ASCD), 145.
8. W. Edwards Deming, *Schools and Communities Cooperating for Quality—Lessons for Leaders* (Alexandria, VA: American Association of School Administrators, 1990), ch. 4, p. 6.
9. "Scores Indicate Lack of Elementary Science Lessons," *Oakland (CA) Tribune* (9 December 2001), 3N.
10. Robert Marzano, *What Works in Schools* (Alexandria, VA: ASCD, 2003), 114.
11. Ibid., 109.
12. Reeves, *The Leader's Guide to Standards,* 10.
13. Michael Clay Thompson, *Classics in the Classroom* (Unionville, NY: Royal Fireworks Press, 1995), 31.
14. Ventures for Excellence, Dr. Vic Cottrell, president, located in Lincoln, Nebraska.
15. Pedro A. Noguera, "Transforming High Schools," *Educational Leadership* (May 2004): 29.
16. Greg Hutchins, "Learn Lean," *Quality Progress* (September 2001): 97.

Chapter 8

1. Peter Senge, *The Fifth Discipline* (New York: Doubleday, 1990), 219–20.
2. Phillip Schlechty, *Shaking up the Schoolhouse* (San Francisco: Jossey-Bass, 2001).
3. Dennis Drenner, *The Washington Post* (11 March 2003): A8.
4. Deann Smith, "Incentive Package to Reward Students for Test Scores," *The Kansas City Star* (8 April 2003). www.kansascity.com/mld/kansascity/news/local/5490692.htm.
5. Associated Press, "Chicago Schools to Get Cash Reward," *The Kansas City Star* (30 October 2002). www.kansascity.com/mld/kansascity/news/nation/4403568.htm.
6. Fran Spielman and Rosalind Rossi, "Schools Offer Prizes for Attendance," *Chicago Sun-Times* (13 August 2003). Suntimes.com
7. Michelle R. Davis, "Department Picks 11 Sites for Reading Program," *Education Week* (5 May 2004): 34.
8. Senge, 340.
9. Associated Press, "Scoring Error Sends Cash to Wrong Schools," *Contra Costa Times* (29 September 2001): A14.
10. Stephen C. Lundin, Harry Paul, and John Christensen, *Fish* (New York: Hyperion, 2000), 2.
11. Jim Collins, *From Good to Great* (New York: HarperCollins, 2001), 10.
12. Edward Deci, *Why We Do What We Do* (New York: Penguin Books, 1995), 47–48.
13. Collins, *From Good to Great*, 74.
14. David Elkind, *Children and Adolescents*, 2nd ed. (New York: Oxford University Press, 1974), 51.
15. Michael Clay Thompson, *Classics in the Classroom* (Unionville, NY: Royal Fireworks Press, 1995), 60.
16. Ibid., 24.
17. Shelly Carson, *Continuous Improvement in the History and Social Science Classroom* (Milwaukee: ASQ Quality Press, 2000) and Jeff Burgard, *Continuous Improvement in the Science Classroom* (Milwaukee: ASQ Quality Press, 2000).
18. Pedro A. Noguera, "Transforming High Schools," *Educational Leadership* (May 2004): 31.
19. John G. Conyers and Robert Ewy, *Charting Your Course* (Milwaukee: ASQ Quality Press, 2003), 113.
20. Oswald Chambers, *My Utmost for His Highest* (Uhrichsville, OH: Barbour Publishing, 1935), February 11.
21. Collins, *From Good to Great*, 177.
22. Lundin, Paul, and Christensen, *Fish*, 66.
23. Leslie Hart, *Human Brain and Human Learning* (New York: Longman, 1983), 74.

24. Deci, *Why We Do What We Do,* 86.

25. Robert Marzano, *What Works in Schools* (Alexandria, VA: ASCD, 2003), 144.

Chapter 9

1. Douglas Reeves, *The Leader's Guide to Standards* (San Francisco: Jossey-Bass, 2002), 26.
2. Peter Senge, *The Fifth Discipline* (New York: Doubleday, 1990), 356.
3. Reeves, *The Leader's Guide to Sandards,* 70–71.
4. Michael Clay Thompson, *Classics in the Classroom* (Unionville, NY: Royal Fireworks Press, 1995), 70.
5. Reeves, *The Leader's Guide to Sandards,* 217.
6. Thomas R. Guskey, "Making the Grade: What Benefits Students?" *Educational Leadership* 52, no. 2 (1994): 14.
7. Robert Marzano, *What Works in Schools* (Alexandria, VA: ASCD, 2003), 37.
8. QI Macros, a software company located in Denver, Colorado.

Chapter 10

1. Richard DuFour, "What Is a Professional Learning Community?" *Educational Leadership* (May 2004): 8.
2. Douglas Reeves, *The Leader's Guide to Standards* (San Francisco: Jossey-Bass, 2002), 117.
3. Lloyd Dobyns and Clare Crawford-Mason, *Thinking About Quality* (New York: Times Books of Random House, 1994), 170.
4. Phillip C. Schlechty, *Shaking Up the Schoolhouse* (San Francisco: Jossey-Bass, 2001), 19.
5. Jim Collins, *From Good to Great* (New York: HarperCollins, 2001), 72.
6. Reeves, *Leader's Guide,* 66.
7. Myron Tribus, "Selected Papers on Quality and Productivity Improvement" (Washington DC: National Society of Professional Engineers): 33.

Further Insights

1. James W. Guthrie and Ray Petty, "Intellectual Capital: Australian Annual Reporting Practices," *Journal of Intellectual Capital* 1, no. 3 (2000): 241–51.
2. Lee Jenkins, *Improving Student Learning: Applying Deming's Quality Principles in the Classroom* (Milwaukee: ASQC Quality Press, 1997).
3. Lee Jenkins, *Improving Student Learning through Data,* In-service presented at Oklahoma City Public Schools (Oklahoma City, OK, January 1999).
4. Lee Jenkins, *Improving Student Learning: Applying Deming's Quality Principles in the Classroom,* 2nd ed. (Milwaukee: ASQ Quality Press, 2003).
5. Lloyd O. Roettger, *The Pursuit of Quality in the Academy.* Paper presented at the fall conference of the Rocky Mountain Educational Research Association; in Edmond, Oklahoma, November 2002.

6. Lee Jenkins, *Improving Student Learning*.
7. Joe Agron, "Status Quo." *American School & University* 1, Article 6 (1997). Retrieved January 28, 2004, from http://asumag.com/ar/university_status_quo/index.htm.
8. W. Edwards Deming. Quote from January, 2002 conference sponsored by American Association of School Administrators, Washington, D.C.
9. Jackie "Moms" Mabley (Speaker), *At the UN*, Chess Records, LP-1452, 1961, phonograph record.
10. Caroline J. Roettger, and Dave Stamps, *Reaching for the Stars: Continuous Improvement Strategies in the Classroom Using Data for Decision Making* (Oklahoma City, OK: Office of Grants, Oklahoma City Public Schools, 2002). Vision Production Public and Community Services College of Continuing Education University of Oklahoma. DVD.
11. Sharon B. Merriam and Rosemary S. Caffarella, *Learning in Adulthood: A Comprehensive Guide,* 2nd ed. (San Francisco: Jossey-Bass, 1999).
12. David V. Williams and Lloyd O. Roettger, "Applying the Right Psychology to Adult Learners at Tinker Air Force Base Skills Center." Central Forum 3, no. 3 (2002): 16–25.

Appendix A

1. John Dew, "The Seven Deadly Sins of Quality Management," *Quality Progress* (September 2003): 59.
2. Ibid., 59.
3. Dave Nelson, "To Find the Root Cause, That's Why," *Quality Progress* (September 2003): 104.
4. Dean L. Gano, *Apollo Root Cause Analysis* (Yakima, WA: Apollonian Publications, 2003).

About the Author

Lee Jenkins, PhD, authored *Improving Student Learning: Applying Deming's Quality Principles in Classrooms,* First and Second Edition and edited the *Continuous Improvement in the Classroom* series for Quality Press. In addition he authored or co-authored *It's a Tangram World, Let's Pattern Block It, Coin Stamp Mathematics, Fraction Tiles, The Balance Book, Geoblocks and Geojackets,* and *Math Manipulatives (Using the Ellison Letter Cutter.)*

Lee works full time as an author, speaker, and consultant. He is the principal consultant for From LtoJ Consulting Group, Inc. and a From LtoJ Software, LLC partner. Both corporations are located in Scottsdale, Arizona.

Lee served in the public schools of California for 30 years, taught part time at several universities and taught full time at Oregon State University from 1978–1983. Lee is a member of the American Society for Quality, the Association for Curriculum Development and Supervision, the American Association of School Administrators, and the National Staff Development Council.

Lee's degrees are from Point Loma Nazarene University, California State University, San Jose, and The Claremont Graduate University. He and his wife Sandy recently celebrated their 40th anniversary.

Lee can be contacted via e-mail at lee@fromltoj.com, or phone 480-634-4059. His Web address is: www.fromltoj.com.

Information on From LtoJ Software is available at www.fromltoj.com or contact Donna Floyd, President, ddfloyd@fromltoj.com, phone 480-577-6835.

The charts shown in Figures 2.3, 2.4, 2.10, 2.11, and 8.6 are created and produced by From LtoJ Software, LLC, and reproduced herein for publication.

Index